THE EMPTY CHAIR

THE EMPTY CHAIR
Tales from Gestalt Therapy

Vikram Kolmannskog

Routledge
Taylor & Francis Group
LONDON AND NEW YORK

Translated by Vikram Kolmannskog and Jonathan Fraenkel-Eidse.

This book was first published in Norwegian as *Den tomme stolen: Fortellinger fra gestaltterapi* by Flux forlag in October 2015, Oslo, Norway.

The English edition has been slightly revised from the Norwegian.

First published 2018
by Routledge
2 Park Square, Milton Park, Abingdon, Oxon OX14 4RN

and by Routledge
711 Third Avenue, New York, NY 10017

Routledge is an imprint of the Taylor & Francis Group, an informa business

Copyright © 2018 by Vikram Kolmannskog

The right of Vikram Kolmannskog to be identified as author of this work has been asserted by him in accordance with sections 77 and 78 of the Copyright, Designs and Patents Act 1988.

All rights reserved. No part of this book may be reprinted or reproduced or utilised in any form or by any electronic, mechanical, or other means, now known or hereafter invented, including photocopying and recording, or in any information storage or retrieval system, without permission in writing from the publishers.

Trademark notice: Product or corporate names may be trademarks or registered trademarks, and are used only for identification and explanation without intent to infringe.

British Library Cataloguing-in-Publication Data
A catalogue record for this book is available from the British Library

Library of Congress Cataloging-in-Publication Data
A catalog record has been requested for this book

ISBN: 978-1-78220-613-2 (pbk)

Typeset in Palatino LT Std
by Medlar Publishing Solutions Pvt Ltd, India

*To Daan van Baalen, my former therapist,
former teacher, and current colleague.
Thank you.*

CONTENTS

ABOUT THE AUTHOR   ix

PREFACE   xi

CHAPTER ONE
What is gestalt therapy?   1

CHAPTER TWO
Succeeding at everything, even stressing less   17

CHAPTER THREE
Three generations of betrayal   29

CHAPTER FOUR
Marianne's memories   43

CHAPTER FIVE
Inside the walls   69

CHAPTER SIX
Put on your own mask first					81

CHAPTER SEVEN
Freeze							97

CHAPTER EIGHT
The bearded lady					113

CHAPTER NINE
The empty chair						129

NOTES							151

REFERENCES						163

INDEX							171

ABOUT THE AUTHOR

Vikram Kolmannskog is a gestalt therapist and writer based in Oslo, Norway. He has a private practice, and teaches and researches as associate professor at the Norwegian Gestalt Institute. He has also trained as a lawyer with specialisation in human rights, and as a social scientist with a doctoral degree in sociology of law.
    www.Vikram.no

PREFACE

"I don't know"
—Dalai Lama

My mother and I share a long-standing interest in the fourteenth Dalai Lama, Tenzin Gyatso, his life and teachings. In 2011, we went to Copenhagen to hear him speak. Much of the journey and experience was about my relationship with my mother, the shared experience, the joy and community with the others who came. Out of what the Dalai Lama said, there is one sentence that has remained with me. At some point, someone asked him a question. I don't remember what. He was quiet for a moment. Then he said, "I don't know." And then there was silence for a few seconds again. If the Dalai Lama can say that he doesn't know, I guess I can as well. I don't have to pretend. In the sentence I took back from Copenhagen lies a much needed honesty and recognition of imperfection. I also like to think that implicit in the three words are a cultivated uncertainty and a curiosity and openness to others and the world. These are fundamental attitudes in gestalt therapy as well.

I am a gestalt therapist. In this book I have collected some stories based on different cases from my practice. Both in form and substance they are in line with gestalt therapy: they are based on sense impressions, bodily sensations, feelings and thoughts that I became aware of when meeting different clients. And they are written as dialogues. An aware, dialogical approach is both a method and a goal of gestalt therapy. Through awareness and dialogue we can experience more of ourselves, the other, and the world. We become more whole. And that is a good definition of "health" and "healing", to become more whole.

This book is for you with an interest in therapy and how we can reduce unnecessary suffering. A series of challenges in our societies are addressed through the individual stories, such as stress, abuse, isolation, bullying, and restrictive gender norms. As a gestalt therapist, I recognise the importance of change on personal, group and societal levels.

Although this is first and foremost a collection of stories, the book can also be an introduction to gestalt therapy for everyone who is curious as well as provide some perspectives for more experienced therapists. The introductory chapter gives an overview of the history of gestalt therapy and discusses some central concepts. Reflections about the therapy and choices I make as a therapist are found in each story as part of my inner dialogue or as expressed in dialogue to the client. In addition, certain phenomena and processes are commented upon in a separate section following each story.

The book is influenced by my training at, and affiliation with, the Norwegian Gestalt Institute. Being a human rights lawyer, social scientist and practitioner of Buddhist meditation also colours my therapeutic approach. In addition, I draw on other disciplines and concepts that have come to dominate current mental health thinking, including mindfulness and the understanding of trauma. Hence, this is gestalt therapy as I understand and practise it.

In the stories, I don't describe what happened and what was said in therapy as precisely as possible. Details have been altered to protect privacy. Furthermore, I have taken some creative licence and made use of literary devices in order for the stories to work better as stories. I would like to thank all my clients—both those whose stories I build on here but also everyone else—for our sessions together. I would also like to thank family, friends, colleagues, and the Norwegian and British publishers for all their support.

CHAPTER ONE

What is gestalt therapy?

Laura's life—and one version of gestalt therapy's history

During the autumn of 1926, psychology student Lore Posner attended a lecture at Frankfurt University.[1] The renowned professor Kurt Goldstein and Adhemar Gelb were talking about their research within gestalt psychology. This subject addresses how we sense and interpret our impressions. What our awareness is drawn to in certain situations and which meanings we apply to what we are aware of varies from person to person. This can also be connected to phenomenology, an understanding and appreciation of people understanding something—a phenomenon—in their particular way. The phenomenon is not only determined by what exists out there, but also through bodily, emotional and thought processes. Yet, with training we can perceive more clearly what is novel in a situation, colouring it less with our expectations, comparisons, and old mindsets.

In addition, according to gestalt psychologists we organise our impressions in agreement with some general principles. For example, something may emerge—as a figure—against a (back)ground. An example of figure-ground perception is Rubin's vase. Either you see a vase, or you see two faces. The figure-ground perception can among other things be influenced by previous experiences and the needs of the situation here and now. Often we can also actively alternate between what figure we notice—a vase or two faces in our example—but both cannot be seen at the same time. Together the parts create a meaningful whole—a "Gestalt" in German.

Goldstein wanted to develop this further and use gestalt principles on the human organism's organisation of itself and their surroundings. But, at one point during the lecture in Frankfurt, Lore became bored. She looked around and noticed a man in his early thirties. "I didn't know who he was. I had the feeling: 'There he is!'" she later recounted. Using gestalt psychology terminology, we can say that the young man became figure and Goldstein and Gelb a part of the ground.

One version of Rubin's vase.

The twelve-years-older Friedrich, better known as Fritz, had been in the trenches during the First World War, trained as a doctor, and now worked as Goldstein's research assistant. "I was very young, naive and inexperienced … yah, he was very impressive," Lore later said. These two would come to share some good and many difficult years together. They would become the founders of a new form of therapy, gestalt therapy, one which was influenced by their lives, the people around them, and the ideas at the time.

In addition to gestalt psychology, both Lore and Fritz had an interest in Sigmund Freud and psychoanalysis from early on. They went for analysis and eventually became psychoanalysts themselves. It was especially the less orthodox, such as Karen Horney and Wilhelm Reich, who appealed to them. Fritz was client to both. With Reich, it was not enough to simply lie on the couch and talk. Reich believed that who we are and what we are struggling with is expressed bodily here and now through our posture, movements, and such. Lore also became engaged with body-oriented approaches such as the Feldenkrais and Alexander methods. While Freud's psychoanalysis was described as the "talking-cure", the gestalt therapists would devote as much attention to the bodily expressions and form as to the content of what clients talked about. Moreover, rather than the subconscious, the past and the therapist's expert role as analyst, gestalt therapists would emphasise what the therapist and client could be aware of here and now and share through dialogue.

More than any of the gestalt psychologists and the psychoanalysts, it was the existential philosopher and theologian Martin Buber who influenced Lore, according to Lore herself. At one point he was her lecturer. She also counted him among her friends, and she was impressed with the way he—in her words—"respected people". According to Buber, the I does not exist in itself, but only as part of the relation "I-It" or "I-Thou".[2] I can relate to the other as an object or a means, one that I will do something with, an It. I can also relate to the other as the other is here and now. I and Thou can then meet in dialogue as whole people. The gestalt therapists' view of relationships in general, and the therapist-client relationship in particular, was influenced by these thoughts. Lore and Fritz also had other existentialists in their social circle, and in gestalt therapy we find ideas such as the meaning of each person's life not being already given, but instead constantly created by the person in interaction with others, that we all experience and must live with imperfection, and that everything and everyone are impermanent.

Eastern worldviews and practices such as Zen and Tao also became important for Lore and Fritz. Much of it fit well with ideas from gestalt psychology and existentialism. For example, in Zen one is concerned with awareness and what is here and now, including sense impressions, bodily sensations, feelings and thoughts. Through awareness training

Zen practitioners can experience a situation as new, and be less confined by old mindsets and habitual reactions. Due to the Zen influence, there are some common elements between gestalt therapy and mindfulness-based therapies that have recently become popular. There are also important differences, however, including the gestalt emphasis on dialogical relationship and creative exploration.

Art and literature were central for Lore and Fritz. Since the age of five, Lore played the piano. From the age of eight she practised modern dance. Fritz was especially interested in theatre and performed in plays by Max Reinhard. Later, many people would warmly recount how they danced with Lore and role-played with Fritz—both within and outside the therapy room. Right from its beginnings, gestalt therapy has encouraged creativity in the exploration of what is here and now.

With great sadness, Lore would later describe how they would have to sell all of their books—thousands of them—for next to nothing and flee. Like other political dissidents and Jews like Goldstein, Freud, Reich, and Buber, they decided to flee when Hitler and the Nazis came to power. "We lost everything, our library, everything." First they fled to Amsterdam, but there were already many refugees there and they were unable to get working permits, so they had to journey onwards. In retrospect this proved to be a blessing in disguise, as many of those who remained there were killed. "My sister, her family who lived in Holland, all died."

Lore, Fritz and their young daughter travelled onwards to South Africa. "We were terribly in love with each another and the baby. [T]hose were very good years." Yet it soon became more difficult. When Lore became pregnant with their son, they had a big argument. Fritz felt that it was too much with two children alongside their therapy practice and research. Over time, he showed less and less interest in the children. Then came the rupture with the orthodox psychoanalysts. At a conference, Fritz held a presentation that was considered to go against the correct Freudian teaching. (The presentation, by the way, was largely based on Lore's experiences as a mother, but it was only Fritz who was credited as author to the presentation and the book that was later published.[3]) Intellectually, they now felt even more banished and alone. Eventually the political situation in South Africa also worsened with the establishment of apartheid. "[F]aced with the 48' elections we didn't want to be there anymore," Lore later recounted.

They moved to the USA, and Lore became Laura. In New York they found many like-minded people such as the anarchist philosopher, social critic and author Paul Goodman. Moreover, he was openly bisexual, something quite rare at the time. His critique of the current competitive and consumer society as well as his work for more inclusive, meaningful relationships and societies would influence gestalt therapy. According to Laura, he deserves to be counted as the third founder of the therapy form: "[W]ithout him there would be no theory of gestalt therapy." Even though Fritz and an American psychology professor, Ralph Hefferline, are named first as authors, it is assumed that Paul Goodman was behind much of the theory in *Gestalt Therapy: Excitement and Growth in the Human Personality*.[4] The book was published in 1951 and is considered the foundational text of gestalt therapy.

Immediately after the publication, Laura, Fritz and Paul established the first gestalt institute. "[I]t was really then when things started to gel. Up until then what we were doing didn't have any name," Laura later recounted. There had in fact been much discussion about the name itself.[5] When Fritz suggested "gestalt therapy", Laura objected because she believed that the therapy form now differed too much from the gestalt psychology that she had studied. She personally preferred "existential therapy". In the end Fritz had his way.

The tension between the two increased in other areas as well. Fritz came and went, and had relationships with other women. Soon he was spending most of his time in other parts of the country. In the 1960s, he got a sort of hippie-guru role in California. Laura remained in New York. Over time, differences in their therapeutic approach also became clearer. In retrospect many have described Fritz as rather challenging and Laura as a more supportive therapist.

On the other hand, they did show some care for one another right until the end. On the day of Fritz' death in Chicago in 1970, Laura had tried to call and hear how he was doing, but unsuccessfully. She sat down and listened to the radio. "Odetta sang something and I said, 'Fritz would have liked to have heard that,' and it struck me that I had said it as if he was already dead. And at that moment he died," she recounted later. "I am not a bitter woman. I have gotten over the mourning ... through the years when he came and went ... and came and went, it was always another separation and another period of mourning and resentment. Now it is final. I have lived through it and I think I am over it. I am also more creative." Elsewhere she writes that true creativity is closely linked to awareness and being conscious of our mortality. "The sharper this awareness, the greater the urge to bring forth something new, to participate in the infinitely continuing creativeness in nature".

Laura continued to practise and teach gestalt therapy. For a long time, it was Fritz' 1960s version of the therapy that dominated the image most people had of gestalt therapy, but over time many have discovered Laura's and Paul Goodman's contributions and increasingly emphasised these. Over the years, institutions have been established across the world. The Norwegian Gestalt Institute has educated hundreds of therapists and other gestalt practitioners since 1986, and is now a well-recognised university college. Laura also travelled abroad and held seminars in Germany, among other places. In 1990, she died close to Frankfurt, in the place where she had been born eighty-five years earlier, in the country she had fled from fifty-seven years earlier. In a way, the circle was complete. Exile and home, life and death; these too are meaningful wholes, great gestalts.

"I and Thou, here and now"

Rubin's vase is a good symbol for gestalt therapy. You can see two faces that are turned towards one another and imagine that they are in dialogue. You can also become aware of more in a situation when you are together with another person: maybe one person notices the faces in the image and can help the other see them, while the other may help the first person to also see the vase. An aware, dialogical approach is gestalt therapy's overarching method as well as goal. As such, the therapy form has also been summarised as "I and Thou, here and now".[6] The ideas about relating borrow from Buber's dialogical philosophy. The ideas about awareness borrow especially from gestalt psychology, phenomenology, and Zen.

In *Gestalt Therapy* by Perls, Hefferline, and Goodman, as well as other English-language gestalt literature, much is written about "awareness".[7] This entails a whole and intimate experience of what is here and now. In line with gestalt psychology, many gestalt therapists call that which we have our focused awareness on the "figure". While certain therapeutic forms are primarily concerned with our thoughts, others our feelings, and others still so-called body-oriented, gestalt therapy is a holistic approach to the person and personal experience. One can be aware through and of bodily sensations, feelings, thoughts, and sense impressions. Awareness of what is here and now also includes what we do and how we do it in relation with others, how we affect and are affected in a particular situation.

As a gestalt therapist I try to support and strengthen the client's awareness. I do this by being aware of myself, the client, and our shared situation. I listen to and respond to the content of what the client shares. At the same time, I focus on the form and the process. I can become aware of something external, such as the client's movements, gaze, and tone of voice. I can become aware of my own bodily sensations such as an increased pulse or heavy breathing when meeting the client. I can become aware of my own feelings such as irritation, sadness or happiness when meeting the client. This is the most basic information I have access to in the situation. When I share some of this, the client can become more aware of themselves, me, how we affect and are affected by one another and the situation we are a part of.

I am also aware of my own thoughts. They may take the form of an inner dialogue. They include professional reflections about the situation with the client and therapeutic choices. They also include more personal experiences. Ideally, I will alternate between awareness of this, awareness of my own bodily sensations and feelings, and awareness of the client and our situation here and now. Sometimes I will try to put thoughts aside to see more clearly what emerges between us here and now. If I believe that it may be useful, based on my total awareness, I may also choose to share some of my thoughts with the client. I can check if what I am saying rings true for the client or not, and respect the client's answer, their subjective reality and truth. By asking, or when the client shares something about themselves on their own initiative, I can also learn more about the client's awareness, including bodily sensations, feelings, thoughts, and what the client senses externally.

Unfinished business

With good descriptions of what is here and now, attempts at historical explanations and interpretations become less important. This does not mean that I do not care about the past and future, but I focus on how these manifest here and now through our contact, the client's memories, worries, expectations, bodily sensations, and so on. Certain powerful experiences from the past can definitely dominate new relationships and situations.

One day at a restaurant, Kurt Lewin, a gestalt psychologist and social psychologist, was struck by how well a waiter remembered the details of an order, but then forgot these once the bill had been paid. This triggered Lewin's curiosity, and his student Bluma Zeigarnik conducted a research experiment.[8] The tendency to better remember uncompleted tasks than completed ones became known as the Zeigarnik effect.

This idea has influenced the gestalt concepts of "unfinished situations" and "unfinished business".[9] Sometimes we can have an experience of having lacked something—for example, care—or of not having finished something ourselves, such as come to terms with something or someone. Important unfinished situations or unfinished business can affect us and our awareness in new situations until we feel we have finished in one way or another. We can also understand this as "fixation", or a "fixed gestalt", in that the unfinished continues to figure in new situations.

There are some parallels between these concepts and the concept of "trauma", which etymologically means wound. Many gestalt therapists are today concerned with trauma and trauma treatment. By supporting and strengthening our clients' awareness, we believe that they can close or finish the old—at least to some degree—and experience also what is new in the situation here and now.

Paradoxical change

Some therapists belonging to other traditions emphasise the client's need to replace negative thoughts with other thoughts in order to achieve change. Others try to get the client to act in a particular manner. Others still interpret the client and express these interpretations in the hope that this can lead to change. Such approaches may involve what Buber refers to as the I-It relationship: the therapist perceives the client as an object—a diagnosis or a problem that needs solving—and as a means, since through solving the problem the therapist can feel successful. The client in turn perceives the therapist as a means, an expert, and a solution, something that can change them. Maybe the client sees themselves as an object, a diagnosis or problem, a thing that must be changed.

While there will be elements of the I-It relationship in gestalt therapy as well, the therapy form ideally involves a greater degree of what Buber calls the I-Thou relationship and dialogue. I try to be aware of the client as a whole person. I try to see things from the client's perspective and support their awareness of what is here and now. At the same time, I am aware of myself as a whole person. I am present in the dialogue as who I am, instead of trying to be anything else. In gestalt therapy, professionalism is linked to awareness and the ability to reflect based on gestalt theory. I both can and should be personal and professional at the same time. Dialogue means that I too am open and vulnerable. I both affect and am affected.

Through aware, dialogical relationships change can occur. Many of us have become so accustomed to others and ourselves trying to force us to become something else than what we are here and now, that we have come to believe that this is necessary for change. Yet in gestalt therapy change can be understood as a paradoxical process: "… change occurs when one becomes what he [sic] is, not when he [sic] tries to become what he [sic] is not" (Beisser, 1970, unpaginated). This is known as the paradoxical theory of change.

Often it is our attempts to push ourselves and others to become something else that leads to stagnation, shame, and unnecessary suffering. When I as a therapist take an aware, dialogical approach, something new can happen. Maybe the client becomes aware of something. Spontaneous change can occur. Maybe it also becomes possible for the client to respond consciously instead of reacting automatically to the situation. Fritz Perls often spoke about responsibility as "response-ability", that is, the ability to respond.[10] Maybe the client also takes a more aware, dialogical approach to themselves and to others.

In contact

"[I]t is the contact that is the simplest and first reality", according to the authors of *Gestalt Therapy* (Perls, Hefferline, & Goodman, 1951, p. 3). One example they use to illustrate this is that it makes no sense to talk about someone who breathes without considering air as part of their definition. Nature, social relationships, culture, and politics are important and inherent factors in a person's life. From the start, gestalt therapists have been concerned with the person as a part of a situation and larger context, instead of studying individuals in isolation.

While some therapists talk about defence mechanisms, resistance, disturbances, and interruptions, many gestalt therapists today prefer the concept "contact styles".[11] This implies an understanding that we always are in contact with something or someone, that we have different ways of being in contact and that none of them are absolutely positive or negative in themselves. Because the contact style is something that happens between us, not something the client creates alone, it is also necessary to be aware of what my contribution is as well as the client's. Using the contact styles we can describe many relational qualities, perhaps more nuances of Buber's I-It and I-Thou relationships.

"Introjection" refers to a person taking in advice, norms and other messages from the surroundings. Much of this typically occurs with little consciousness. The metaphor often used is that one swallows something whole without first chewing. This can be important in some learning. Yet it can also result in inner, self-critical voices and a heavy burden of "shoulds", "musts", and "oughts". Introjection is expressed in the stories included here as "we should be good parents" and "the body must be kept in shape". One example of internalised oppression is when a client who has experienced sexual abuse says "I'm a whore". The opposite of introjection can be to chew on something and choose whether we want to spit it out or assimilate it as our own—in other words to explore what we ourselves want and are able to do instead of simply experiencing that we should and must.

"Projection" means to throw something out or forth. Often there is something in the other person that makes us project what we do on that precise person. Moreover, imagination and interpretation, including metaphors,[12] are entirely necessary in our attempts to understand the world. However, projection can also overshadow what is novel in new relationships and situations, and it can involve disowning something—what is projected—in oneself. Examples from the stories are "men are unfaithful" and "how brave of you". The opposite of projection can be taking ownership and responsibility for oneself, focusing on sense impressions here and now and checking one's interpretations with the other person. As a therapist I often check my interpretations with the client—and can invite the client to check their interpretations with me.

"Retroflection" implies that one holds oneself back or turns against oneself. We all need impulse control and reflection, but this can also go too far. Physically, retroflection can involve tensing certain muscles, holding the breath or shallow breathing. In the stories we meet a man who holds his stomach in and chest out, a girl who "packs down" and avoids the "lump" in her stomach through shallow breathing, and a young man who holds back by tensing his leg muscles. The opposite of retroflection can be sharing something and expressing oneself to others.

Sometimes disclosing something about myself and my feelings can contribute to the client also sharing more about themselves.

"Deflection" means to bend or turn aside. Deflection is especially clear in the story about the young man who has been bullied and now struggles with his self-esteem. When he receives compliments or is in other ways put in the spotlight, he dodges away by physically moving, changing the topic, focusing on others, and laughing. Deflection is expressed as laughter in several of the other stories as well. Humour and laughter can provide another perspective and physiologically relax us. Deflection has many benefits, but can also have its disadvantages. Sometimes it is necessary to focus and hold on to something.

"Confluence" means flowing together. It can involve empathy, cooperation, simply being together, and support. These qualities are hopefully present in all of the stories. In language it can be expressed through the use of the word "we". But confluence is not unconditionally good either. For example, it can cloud disagreement and conflict. Differentiation between oneself and the other, resistance, protest and isolation can also be necessary. The importance of confluence, differentiation and protest become especially apparent in the story about the client who has experienced sexual abuse and refers to herself as a whore.

These are some of the contact styles that I am especially interested in as a therapist. We can think of many more. I have described each of them separately, but in many situations there are several contact styles that dominate at the same time and they affect each other. And, as should be clear from the above description, they can be organised into poles and counter-poles; for example, introjection-chewing, projection-owning, retroflection-sharing, deflection-focusing, and confluence-differentiation.

Polarities

A "polarity" is a pole and a counter-pole that are complementary and connected, rather than dichotomous and incommensurable. Polarity theory is particularly based on ideas from Tao, such as yin and yang, and gestalt psychology's figure-ground perception. We can only experience yin as a figure with yang as a background, and yang as figure with yin as background. Challenge is possible because support is possible. Differentiation is possible because confluence is possible. Control is possible because letting go is possible. I can control and I can let go.

Polarities can be expressed at many levels, in individuals, couples, groups, and societies. The theory involves an appreciation of human diversity and paradoxical truths about each of us.

Nevertheless, many of us are quite rigid and stereotypical. Some almost always see yang, others yin. Some are often confrontational, others generally supportive. Some differentiate a lot, others are very confluent. Some want total control, others almost let go completely. This may have been the best possible adaptation in a difficult situation in life, but it may have become a fixation over time. We are then less aware and identify ourselves less with certain sides, so-called "blind spots" or "shadow sides" (Zinker, 1977, p. 200).

This can entail inner and interpersonal conflicts and unnecessary suffering. The blind spots or shadow sides do not simply go away. Often they appear as an apologetic and sabotaging "underdog" in a dynamic that ensures that the "top dog" never actually succeeds with their agenda.[13] For example, a client may have experienced that parents or others believe that one should always have control or be controlled. Through introjection, this can lead to a self-criticism and inner conflict with a top dog demanding that one has full control. Through retroflection the shadow side—the counter-pole to control—can be relegated to a part of the body that one is less aware of. And through projection, the conflict can play out between the client and another again—we often project the shadow side onto others. This can become a chain of suffering that we inflict on ourselves and others through generations.

But it is possible to break the chain. Through awareness and dialogue we can become more flexible and whole as people and as societies. To accept the different sides of ourselves and others does not necessarily mean that we should live out all of these sides. In several of the stories the clients describe having a good experience of giving more space to something that is already here, but is rarely accepted in other places.

Above I have provided some examples of polarities. Yet how the polarities form depends on the person and the situation. A pole does not always have one particular counter-pole. In the stories we see, for example, that the counter-pole to control can be sadness, adventurousness, warmth, strength, or something else entirely. As therapist I must be open to whatever might show up. I must also work with my own blind spots and shadow sides.

Experiments

An "experiment" implies that the client and I do something without knowing what the result will be in advance. The goal is first and foremost to explore something together and increase the client's awareness. This differs from other therapy forms where interpretation is central, as well as therapy forms with specific exercises and given goals, where the client should replace negative thoughts with other thoughts and behave in new, specified ways. Additionally, to do something here and now in the form of an experiment is a different experience from merely talking about something that has happened or may happen. One gains a new experience. Afterwards we can share observations and reflect upon what happened and how it was experienced. Perhaps the client recognises something from their own life. Maybe the client becomes inspired to do something new.

Half of the book *Gestalt Therapy* contains experiments that the reader can also participate in.[14] Many gestalt therapists have both written generally about the concept and developed numerous different types of experiments.[15] I build upon many of these. At the same time, the particular experiment arises and is created from my awareness in a concrete situation here and now with a client.

An experiment can be as simple as me sharing something that I have become aware of, mirroring a gesture I have seen or repeating a sentence that I have heard the client say. I can also suggest that the client continues to do something, does more of this—for example exhale or tense the leg muscles—or the opposite and experiences how this is.

Through guided awareness I can ask the client to close their eyes and become aware of what they are experiencing here and now, such as how they are breathing, other bodily sensations, feelings, if there are specific thoughts in the form of images or sentences, etc. A guided fantasy may resemble guided awareness, but in this case I invite the client to mentally enter a particular image, dream, metaphor, or the like.

A number of experiments focus on language. When working with introjection we can try out sentences with "should", "can", and "want". When working with alienation and projection we can experiment with I-statements. For example, I may suggest to a client who says "things exploded last week" to try to say "I exploded". In the story where a client projects being brave, I suggest that the client also tries to say

"I am brave". When working with polarities I may eventually suggest that a client combines the poles in a "both/and" instead of an "either/or" sentence and becomes aware of how this is experienced.

Other experiments involve the body in more obvious ways. For example, we can explore metaphors physically and bodily. In the story about the client who was bullied and struggled with self-esteem, we explore projection—to throw something out—and counter-poles with me physically throwing a pillow at him while I verbally serve him compliments. In another story about a client who struggles with the experience of physical boundaries and body contact, I slowly move closer and ask her when I am close enough or too close.

Some of the most well-known gestalt experiments are so-called "chair work".[16] Fritz Perls developed these based on his interest and knowledge of theatre and psychodrama, a therapy form that uses methods inspired by theatre. In "two-chair work", a client can act out the various needs, desires or sides of themselves in two chairs. While polarities may emerge between myself and the client and can be explored directly in our relationship, I often use chair work in addition. In one chair the client can, for example, play out a desire for control, and perhaps the counter-pole will appear in the other. Often a dialogue develops between the various sides, thereby enabling a better integration of the whole polarity within the client.

"The empty chair" is another version of chair work where the client can imagine a significant person from their life in front of them—for example, an ex who they have not yet let go of. The client can also act out (the projection of) the other in the empty chair, which can result in increased empathy and integration of projected sides. Awareness can increase using chair work, something unfinished can become more finished, something fixed less fixed. A number of studies have shown that chair work has generally good results, and the techniques are now used within several therapy forms, but not necessarily in line with a gestalt approach.[17]

There are virtually no limits to what type of experiments we can use in gestalt therapy as long as they involve trying out something, having an experience, and increasing awareness. This invites creativity and a rich diversity for both gestalt therapists and clients. The experiments in this book are coloured by me and my personal style as well as by the client and our shared situation.

The overarching experiment is always the relationship between the client and myself as therapist.[18] Even when I suggest an experiment, the way I suggest it and the way it is received by the client says something about the client, myself and the situation, and will be an important experiment in itself. Does the client do what I ask without hesitation, or with protests? Does the client go along with doing something unfamiliar, or must everything be under control? Do I become cautious or more directive? Is it actually becoming more of an exercise than an experiment?

Mistakes on my part—often due to a lack of awareness—can also become an opportunity for new experiences and change when I as therapist again become aware and enter into dialogue. In the story about a client with abuse experiences, the client protests about something I do and is met with my respect, me taking responsibility for my mistake, and an apology. This is a new and important experience. That I as therapist am clearly fallible and a whole person can furthermore be an expression of the existential truth of imperfection. To become aware of our common humanity through, among other things, our imperfection can be a means of breaking out of the notion that one is a failure—or a success for that matter—compared to others, an idea that often leads to unnecessary loneliness, shame, and suffering.

This book has also been an experiment. I have, for example, shared drafts of the stories with the various clients. Occasionally, this has led to interesting turns in the therapy—and sometimes to changes in the stories as well.

CHAPTER TWO

Succeeding at everything, even stressing less

Early one winter morning, Carl arrives, a handsome man dressed in a suit. He shakes my hand, takes off his coat and shoes, and we enter the therapy room.

"Where do you want me?" he asks.

Two black chairs, identical, face each other by a window.

"You can choose," I say.

He sits down on one chair, places one leg over the other, and pulls out a notepad. Quick answers and solutions, is that what he wants from me? For a second, there's a tightening in my stomach. Then I smile and sit down—in the same kind of chair as Carl. *I and Thou.*

"As I already mentioned on the phone I've had a burnout and still struggle with stress. I need to learn some stress management, mindfulness."

I remember the phone call when Carl first got in touch. We spent quite some time trying to find time in his busy schedule to meet. Now we have an hour before he has to rush off to the job that he was on sick leave from until recently because of the burnout.

"I remember. And I believe I told you that we could give it a try and see what we can do together. I'm a gestalt therapist and have no specialist training in mindfulness. But awareness of what is here and now is central in gestalt therapy as well, and I practise meditation myself."

"Yes. So how do we do this? I've never been in therapy before."

"We're already doing it." I smile. "We can start by getting to know each other a little bit. And while we sit here talking, we can also try to be aware of what is going on in and between us. Maybe our way of relating to each other can say something about your relations to yourself and others as well. Maybe it can give us some information about stress, burnout, and possible ways out."

There's a tightening around Carl's eyes, his lower forehead. I think he's thinking. He looks at the notepad, puts it down, and looks back at me again. Maybe he's already trying out something new.

For a few seconds there's silence. Now we also need something safe, some talking, I think to myself. "Maybe you want to start by telling me a little bit about yourself and your life?"

"Sure. Where to start? I have a job in finance and a demanding boss to put it mildly. I have three children. There are so many activities and equipment they need, you have no idea. Now it's skiing of course. We have to be good parents. And then I have a wife and friends who must be attended to. The kitchen is being redecorated. Again. And then of course the body has to be kept in shape."

Many *musts* and *shoulds*, I think to myself. This is Carl's world. At the same time, it's increasingly the reality for many of us. Some have described the condition as the thousand internalised demands; others speak of crappy dreams. Surely, these are important ingredients in stress. And what about the relationships? *And then I have a wife and friends who must to be attended to. And the body has to be kept in shape.* I could perhaps reflect these sentences back to Carl to increase awareness of the way he relates to himself and others. On second thought, no, not now; it could be felt as criticism and even more demands. I'll just continue listening for a while. Carl keeps talking. The tempo is quick, the talking itself as well as what he talks about. I sense my breathing becoming shallower and my shoulders stiffening. From what I can see, he's experiencing something similar.

"And the nights, well, I can't really sleep at night." He pauses.

"I hear what you're telling me, Carl, and at the same time I sense my breath changing and shoulders stiffening. My tempo quickens together with you here and now. I can feel stress when you're describing your life."

"You can?"

I nod.

"It's that way for me too. But I seldom take the time to sense what's going on in the body, I guess," he says.

The burden of everything Carl does and thinks he should do is probably heavy. It sure was for me. Eventually it was so heavy I couldn't avoid hearing the stop signals from my body. An image comes to mind now: I'm walking up the street to where I live and work, and I have to stop and rest after every few meters. Shall I say something about this? Maybe it can contribute to a sense of imperfection being something universal. Maybe it can lighten the burden.

"I recognise some of this myself, Carl. I've also experienced burnout."

"Really?"

"It was a few years ago. It was a painful experience. But I did learn to listen more to my body. Before that I had been pushing myself for a long time, been in my head so to speak, focused on all I should and had to do, ignoring the signals from my body."

Carl's experience is unique. So is mine. I have to remember that. At the same time, we are many who have similar experiences today. There is a larger context. I want to recognise that as well with Carl, that it's not just something individual or personal.

"We do live in a particular kind of society, with certain structures and ideas about success and the good life," I continue. "Perhaps burnout is a form of strike, an adaptation to a demanding situation, a signal to ourselves as well as others around us."

Efficiency, productivity, economic growth, consumption, these are some of the norms of our society. And now we have stress management? No, I don't accept that the solution is doing more of the same minus the stress, a sort of McMindfulness. I notice Carl looking at me. He changes position, one leg over the other. I don't know if I can give him what he's asking for, but let's return to the order.

"You mentioned mindfulness. Do you have any previous experience?"

"When I first collapsed and experienced burnout, I bought a pile of books, including some about mindfulness, and quickly read through them."

He is trying to succeed at everything, I think to myself, including stressing less.

"So when you collapsed, you bought a pile of books that you quickly read through." Am I able to reflect this back to him in a friendly and helpful way?

Carl laughs. He has a nice smile, and I smile back. He speaks for many of us. It's good that we can laugh a little at ourselves. It gives perspective. It even reduces a little stress.

"That's me in a nutshell. Quickly looking for a solution, a quick fix."

"Would you like to try some guided awareness here and now?" I suggest.

"Sure." He nods.

"Okay. I'll give some instructions and ask some questions. No need to respond to me. I'm simply guiding you. First, I invite you to close your eyes or rest your gaze on the floor. Just be aware of whatever is happening here and now without needing to change anything. Come home to this moment. What are you aware of? How is your breathing? Become familiar with it as a bodily sensation. Are there other sensations? Just take a moment and be aware of what is." I pause for a while—silence for a few seconds—before continuing: "Is there thinking in the form of mental images or voices? What is the quality of the images or voices? And how do you feel? Is there a particular state of mind?" Again I pause for a few seconds. "Now, you can connect to your breathing again. And then open your eyes. Take a moment to notice what you see and how you see."

Carl looks down at the floor, looks out the window, a tree out there, and then looks at me.

"I feel calm," he says.

"A normal side effect." I smile. "Stress is often connected to a sense that one should be somewhere else or be someone else. Through awareness we can curiously approach what is here and now, regardless of what that is. Feeling more centred and calm is often a result, but not always. And in gestalt therapy the goal of awareness is merely awareness."

"Okay. I'm curious." He places one leg over the other again. "So how do we proceed in the coming sessions?"

Already planning. But yes, how do we proceed? Many mindfulness-based therapies follow a manual with specific exercises. That's probably what Carl is expecting. But is it in line with gestalt therapy's emphasis on the client as a unique person, wholeness and dialogue? Maybe I can adapt a little bit. That would be respectful of his wishes and faithful to a dialogical approach, I guess. We create the therapy together, *I and Thou*.

"I can introduce different exercises in the coming sessions," I suggest. "We could meet once a week for five weeks as a start. Each session could have a different focus. For example, next time we could focus on the breath."

"Sounds good."

"At the same time, this is gestalt therapy, so I would also like us to be open and explore what arises here and now in each session and adjust accordingly," I continue. "I'd also want to focus on our relationship and want us to observe and reflect on what we are doing and how we are doing it together. Now, for example, I think we are planning. How is that for you?"

"It's okay. I like control." He smiles. "But planning too much can also contribute to the stress, I guess. I need to let go a little more, but it costs me a lot."

"And us sitting together here so far, how has that been?"

"It's a little strange sitting here with someone who was a stranger up until just half an hour ago. And just coming to therapy—that felt a little weird."

"So maybe this has been an experience of letting go a little bit?"

"I didn't think of that, but yes, I guess so."

"So you can control and you can let go."

Perhaps Carl and I can experience him as more whole already.

"Yes. Maybe I can."

"And right now, how is it to sit here with me now?"

"It's nice. It's a special space. A world of its own."

"So it was when you were out there, in the other world, that you felt that coming to therapy was a little weird?"

"Yes. You know, what would others say? I haven't told anyone, not even my wife. Don't know if I should."

Other possible ingredients of stress, burnout and suffering more generally, I think to myself, are façade and social comparison. Carl hasn't even told his wife about coming to therapy. I feel something in my chest; sadness, I think.

He looks at me as if wanting advice.

"I don't know," I tell him. I don't want to contribute to more shoulds. "But what I do know, Carl, is that I'm grateful for the trust you show me here and now by talking openly about what you experience as challenging in your life. That is an important step in itself."

"I understood from your webpage that you're a lawyer as well as a therapist. So I guess you work with people in finance and business as well?"

Where did that question come from? Is Carl curious about me as a person? Looking for similarities and differences? I don't want to choose the typical therapist answer now: answering a question by asking a question. I've invited him to focus on our relationship and I want to show myself as an authentic person.

"Most of my time now I spend on therapy—the practice, teaching, and research. But I do some other things as well." I tell him a little bit about my work. In content it's quite different from his; but I also do quite a lot, we have that in common.

"How is it for you to hear me tell you about my life and work, Carl?"

"You do a lot."

"There was even more before, including teaching and practising yoga. Ironically, yoga was one of the activities that contributed to my burnout."

We smile. I'm glad that we can smile at me as well.

"After my burnout, I stopped doing several activities," I continue. "Some of them were linked to social expectations, but others I genuinely enjoyed and was sad to give up. Choices do often entail loss and grief. *Decide* literally means to cut off. It can be brutal. But I also got something back of course: I'm in a much better shape and am more present in the relationships and activities that I've continued with."

Isn't this presentation of my current life a little too rosy? I do less than before, but it's still a lot, perhaps too much. But it's true that I made choices entailing loss and grief. So-called stress management is not sufficient. We also need to recognise existential conditions like choice, loss, grief, and imperfection.

"Do you think it's an individual thing? I mean, I see others around me who are able to do everything, family, work, the gym, everything."

"I wonder what more is in your question, Carl. If I say, 'yes, it's probably an individual thing,' what happens to you?"

"Envy. There's a sense of competition."

"It's good that you become aware of that. And I can understand you. I can feel it myself. At the same time, I think comparisons and competition can be the root of much suffering. And to answer your question: I think people are different, but no one can do everything and not lose anything. Trying to succeed at everything is choosing a stressful life. People's façade on Facebook and elsewhere may indicate differently, but imperfection is universal. When we recognise its universality, imperfection can connect us to each other rather than isolate and stress us. As I mentioned, I myself have cut down on a lot to live with less stress. And yet, I'll admit, I still take on too much sometimes and this results in stress."

I realise we have limited time left, and this reminds me of another existential condition. Remembering death can give another perspective on life. Personally, I experienced burnout as a small death and became more focused on nurturing a few but important relationships and activities in my life.

"What do you want to do with the limited time you have to live? If you take a moment and listen to yourself, your body, your whole being, what is important to you as a person, Carl? And what could you possibly sacrifice?"

"I guess I could make some different choices. Change my job. Buy and live in a smaller, less expensive house. Not change the kitchen every couple of years. Have less activities and things for the children."

The tempo is slower now. There are less shoulds. It's easier to breathe.

"If you want to we can explore this further." He nods. I glance at the clock; still some time, we can make it. Then I sense my heart beating faster. I'm stressing. I also want to perform well, show off what I can do, be a good therapist. But perhaps we can do something different together.

"I'm eager to explore this further here and now. At the same time, I'm aware that we only have a few minutes left of the session and sense the tempo increasing again. So I choose not to. Perhaps we can look at it another time. How is this for you?"

"Well, I was getting a little excited, but at the same time I guess this means we don't have to stress."

There is silence. It's a little pressing. Outside it's snowing.

We talk about the session. We wrap up talking about the weather. Carl picks up his notepad—as empty as when he arrived—leaves the therapy room, puts on his coat and shoes, smiles politely while shaking my hand, and thanks me for the session.

Will he be back? It's unlikely. I could have handled this differently. I should have. I attack and defend myself for a while. Then, I become aware of these thoughts and feelings, and a smile arises. Through awareness we can curiously approach what is here and now, regardless of what that is. I can relate to myself as well with awareness and in a dialogical fashion.

A few weeks later—suddenly it's spring—I receive an email from Carl. He apologises for not getting in touch earlier. He has found a therapist that suits him well and one I can hardly envy: Marka, the forest on the outskirts of Oslo. He goes for daily walks there, mindfulness in Marka. That is what he writes. I get a mental image of Carl walking slowly through the forest. The burden is a little lighter. Then I realise that he's sent me this email, and I'm touched. Maybe our meeting meant something to him after all. I have walked a little stretch with him.

Maybe there are other changes as well. Maybe he's made some new choices, lost and won something. Maybe a smaller house, fewer activities and equipment, but a better relationship with his wife and children. Maybe a not so frequent and hard workout in the gym, but a better relationship to his body and himself. Maybe he's resigned from the job with the demanding boss and earns less, but feels better. I don't know. He doesn't write anything about that. But I'm grateful for his email and the reminder about the healing power of nature.

I look up from the screen and out of the window. A large tree sways lightly and without a sound just outside the therapy room.

"Hi," I whisper and smile.

*　*　*

Comments on "Succeeding at everything, even stressing less"

Stress and burnout: "Stress" is a word with a long history, but the concept, as we understand it today, was first developed by the biologist Hans Selye from the 1930s onwards.[1] Like other animals, human beings have certain physiological reactions to what we perceive as threatening. Fight and flight involve inter alia production of stress hormones, muscle contractions, and increased heartbeat. They have been necessary for our survival. Even when there is not a danger of being killed or anything that requires fight or flight, however, many people in modern societies experience phenomena that are very demanding and put us in a state of almost constant stress. Studies have shown connections between chronic stress and different forms of suffering such as depression and heart diseases.[2] More and more people are experiencing burnout, which is linked to stress and involves a sense of being drained of energy.[3]

The thousand demands and crappy dreams: One definition of psychological stress is that "an individual perceives that environmental demands tax or exceed his or her adaptive capacity" (Cohen, Kessler, & Gordon, 1995 cited in Cohen, Janicki-Deverts, & Miller, 2007, unpaginated). Stress can partly be understood in light of introjection, a too heavy burden of shoulds, of ideals and demands. Modern societies' emphasis on success, looks, availability, exposure and other ideals can be experienced as a "thousand internalised demands" (Gran, 2014, unpaginated; original in Norwegian) according to Norwegian psychologist Sissel Gran. The Swedish feminist and scholar of humanities Nina Björk highlights that political and commercial forces attempt to create in us "crappy dreams" (Björk, 2007, unpaginated; original in Swedish) about kitchen redecoration and other things we really don't need. These may be important ingredients in current introjection and stress. Linked to this are also our ways of relating to ourselves and others, relations often characterised by comparisons, façade, and instrumentality.[4]

Change and existentialism: While much stress can be linked to introjection, there is also much in life that we genuinely want to do. To reduce stress may involve hard choices, loss, and grief. In this story, existential conditions are described and discussed. Existentialists claim that meaning is not given, that we are free to choose, and that this often entails loss, grief, anxiety, and guilt. According to the paradoxical theory, change happens more organically and spontaneously through awareness of what is here and now.[5] These two approaches in gestalt therapy can be complementary and even overlap, but not necessarily. I alternate between the two according to what I believe is needed in a concrete situation with a client.

Humour and laughter: According to the Mayo Clinic, a good laugh can help with stress.[6] This is because we activate and then relax the body through hormones and heart activity. More generally, humour and laughter can play an important role in therapy. The Norwegian psychiatrist Finn Skårderud writes about a movement from ha-ha to aha.[7] He refers to Kant's statement that humour is about putting yourself in a mental position from which things can be viewed differently from how they normally are; Nietzsche's statement about humans so insufferably suffering that they had to invent laughter; and Kierkegaard's words about life being comic due to all its paradoxes and conflicts. Within gestalt therapy, humour can be understood as part of deflection and considered appropriate in many situations: taking another perspective can contribute to new awareness. At other times humour and laughter provide temporary relief and lightness so that an exploration of something difficult and heavy can continue.[8]

McMindfulness or awakening: Mindfulness has its origins in meditation as it was taught by the Buddha and recorded in the Satipatthana Sutta.[9] It can be defined as "the practice of being fully present and alive, body and mind united" (Hahn, 2008, unpaginated). Important elements include a non-judgemental attitude and an awareness of what is here and now, including the breath, other bodily sensations, feelings, and thoughts. Professor of medicine Jon Kabat-Zinn has through extensive research shown its potential for stress reduction and thereby contributed to making the practice recognised within mainstream medicine.[10] Awareness of what is here and now is a common focus of mindfulness-based therapies and gestalt therapy. While mindfulness-based stress reduction (MBSR) and mindfulness-based cognitive therapy (MBCT) are manual-based programmes with certain exercises in sequence administered by a therapist, gestalt therapy is more open, dialogical, and creative. Some have criticised the commercial, secularised version of mindfulness that is increasingly marketed and sold as stress management, a sort of "McMindfulness" (Purser & Loy, 2013). They fear that without the wider social ethics and system of Buddhism, the practice risks maintaining limiting and oppressive processes and structures; we can seemingly go on doing what we are doing, however destructive that is, and perhaps even more, without feeling any stress. The Zen-master Thich Nhat Hanh reminds us, however, that meditation must go hand in hand with social and political engagement: "Meditation is about the awareness of what is going on—not only in your body and in your feelings, but all around you … The practice should address suffering: the suffering within yourself and the suffering around you. They are linked to each other" (Malkin, 2003, unpaginated). This version of mindfulness is more compatible with gestalt therapy with its emphasis on the whole, relationships, and societal and cultural critique—an inheritance from Paul Goodman in particular.

Nature heals: The Zen-master Thich Nhat Hanh is also concerned with our relationship to the natural world: "I think the real miracle is not to walk either on water or in thin air, but to walk on earth. Every day we are engaged in a miracle which we don't even recognise: a blue sky, white clouds, green leaves, the black, curious eyes of a child—our own two eyes" (Hahn, 1999, p. 12). The dialogical philosopher Martin Buber also claimed that we can have profound and important experiences in nature. We can experience a tree as a whole being that we are connected with, as I-Thou, rather than merely a means for us to use for something, as I-It: "It can, however, also come about, if I have both will and grace, that in considering the tree I become bound up in relation to it. The tree is no longer an *It*" (Buber, 2010, p. 7). Holistic awareness, contact and dialogue have been central concepts in gestalt therapy from the start. Still, many gestalt therapists—myself included—have long neglected the human-nature connection and the healing potential that lies therein. This has also been the case for therapists belonging to other traditions. Ecopsychology is a relatively new field seeking to address this.[11] Furthermore, we now have a series of studies that look at the effects of trees and green spaces in cities.[12] For example, people who live in areas with a higher density of trees along the street experience better health, and green spaces can help reduce stress. Simply having a view to a tree—for example through a therapy room window—can help. This kind of awareness, these relationships, can heal individuals and societies with high levels of stress, focus on façade and consumption, control and competition, societies with unhealthy splits between body and mind, nature and humans, societies that are about to destroy large parts of their natural environment and climate and thereby themselves.

CHAPTER THREE

Three generations of betrayal

Through the camera on the Mac, I show Anna the therapy room and the green tree outside. She then shows me a little of where she finds herself, many time zones away. Outside her window the sun is rising over a spectacular skyline; in my therapy room in Oslo it is afternoon.

She sits down on a red sofa and places the Mac on the table in front of her. "Where should I begin?" she says. "It's about infidelity, a partner who was unfaithful to me over many years. But this stretches even further backwards in time. My mother, grandmother, we have all lived with unfaithful men. It's a curse that follows our family or something."

Curse, something she feels she has little control over, something that has been cast upon her and her family. Some sort of ancestral or original sin? Infidelity is quite common. But Anna feels that it has struck her family particularly. Since Freud's time there has been talk of the transmission of specific patterns in certain families through generations. Now there is also much talk about transmission of trauma. And infidelity can be a trauma. In any case, Anna has experienced infidelity directly herself, and indirectly through her mother and grandmother. She has probably heard stories. Maybe she was affected by their ways of relating to themselves and to others. I exhale and exit my thoughts again. I see Anna more clearly, her blonde hair and her smile.

"I've been single for several years now and find relationships difficult. When I was out in a bar last week, I met a man and went home with him. I saw a lot of girl things there and became a little suspicious. He said that they were his ex-girlfriend's things. We were both quite drunk. In the morning I panicked, woke him up, and asked him about the things again before fleeing the place. He must have thought I was completely crazy," she says with a laugh.

Then something happens with the connection. I had said that Skype is not optimal when she first got in touch by email. I told her that there are many good therapists where she lives. It was Anna who insisted; who wanted to speak Norwegian. And she wanted me specifically based on a recommendation from a friend; that's a little flattering of course. I look at the screen, frozen laughter, fixed gestalt. She looks ridiculous. I have to smile. But then I feel something in my chest. I don't think that you're crazy, Anna. I can understand the suspicion. It's not strange after having experienced infidelity. It can be important for a sense of control. And that a man is possibly unfaithful may be an appropriate projection. *A lot of girl things, a little suspicious.* But the old experience and way of relating to men can also be disrupting and make it harder to experience what's novel, here and now.

"Hello?" she says.

The image is moving again. She is not laughing.

"Yes. Hi. It must have gotten stuck," I reply.

"Yeah. That's ironic, because in a way that's what I'm experiencing, I guess, that something is stuck, something from the past that's disturbing the present. Where was I?"

"He must have thought you were completely crazy," I say.

"Right. Actually, that was what my ex claimed as well. You're crazy; this is just something you've made up in your head. That was his reply when I began asking him if there were other women. I felt that the relationship had not been going well for quite a while. But I doubted myself as well, especially when he called me crazy and said that it was only my own nonsense. Maybe it was just my own suspicion, you know. I have undoubtedly been influenced by the stories from my mother and grandmother. Anyways, one day I checked his email and had my fears confirmed. I confronted him again. Eventually he realised that I had been in his email. He was furious. In the end it was Dylan who ended it with me."

He was furious. Not she. Her voice also sounds controlled. Certainly, Anna is sharing something important from her life, but I get a feeling that she is moderating herself and holding back a lot of feeling. At any rate, it certainly hasn't *ended* yet.

"I usually mention this story when I get into a new relationship," she continues. "It's a part of my history. At the same time, I wonder if it's a bad idea to give him so much space."

Yes, I think immediately, a bad idea. Her need for control and this story may have become a fixation. Yet this is just a thought I have, I think to myself, not an objective truth. Better to explore how she feels here and now, to clarify that she is giving him space here with me as well.

"I don't know. With me as well—a new relationship—you now give him space. Dylan."

"Yes."

"I see that something is happening with your eyes, Anna, with your entire face now."

"It hurts. I'm sad. A part of me doesn't want to talk about him."

"We can explore these sides more if you want, the one that doesn't want to talk about him and the one that brings up the story whenever you enter new relationships."

"Okay."

"Then let's try a version of what we call chair work in gestalt therapy. You're now sitting roughly in the middle of the sofa, so I suggest that these two sides of you can be enacted on either end of the sofa respectively. This way each side may become a little clearer to us. Imagine that you are completely entering each of these sides when you physically move. When you feel that the other side is emerging, switch places and talk from that side."

She pushes back the laptop a little so that I can see the whole sofa in the camera, and sits down on one end.

I observe Anna on the red sofa through the camera. She's silent, but it looks as though a lot is happening emotionally. She's sitting hunched over, the long blonde hair falling forward. Her face is slightly tense.

"You look like you are about to cry," I say. "What do you feel? What does this side in you have to say?"

"I'm sad. I want to erase him from my life," she replies with a low voice. Several short, quiet sentences follow.

Then, suddenly, she moves over to the other side of the sofa and straightens up. "But one must simply deal with one's history. You're another experience richer." This is followed by several *ones* and *musts* and *shoulds*.

She alternates a few times between the two sides.

"Maybe that is enough for now," I say after a while. "You can return to the middle of the sofa and we can talk about what just happened."

Anna moves back to the middle, adjusts the laptop and looks at me through the camera again.

"You began with the sad side," I say. "Then, you quickly moved over to the other side where there were many *ones* and *musts* and *shoulds*, the side that claimed that *one must simply deal with one's history*."

"I guess I've spent little time in the sad side and a lot in the other."

"In gestalt therapy we sometimes say that we all have a top dog and an underdog. Maybe the sad side is some sort of underdog, while the other side with all of the imperatives is a more controlling top dog. It's easy to think that it's the top dog that's in charge, but if the underdog is ignored, this side will continue to sabotage things for the top dog. Change happens when you become who you are here and now, when you also allow yourself to be sad," I say.

"That makes sense. It was actually quite good to feel the other side as well, to give that some space."

"I've been sad and thinking a lot since the last session," she tells me the next time we talk. "Thinking about how this has gone on for generations," she says, making a circular gesture with her hand.

"What is that?" I ask, mirroring the gesture with my hand.

"A hamster wheel. I'm stuck. And I want to jump off of it."

Curse, hamster wheel. I like her creative use of language. Maybe we can explore further this latest image of how she experiences the situation.

"I've got an idea, Anna. Do you want to come along on a guided fantasy and explore the hamster wheel further?"

"Um. Okay."

"If you feel okay with it, you can close your eyes and imagine a hamster wheel and yourself. Sense what it's like to be you in the hamster wheel."

Anna sits on the red sofa with eyes closed. "I sense my heart beating. I'm a bit scared," she says.

Am I challenging her too much? I'm not there if she needs me. She did seem slightly uncertain when I suggested the experiment. She says that she's a bit scared now. No, I think it's fine. That she's able to tell me what's happening with her is reassuring. And I am here even if I am not with her physically there.

"It's great that you sense the body's signals so clearly. Simply continue to be aware of whatever is happening and how you feel. I'm here with you. If it becomes too uncomfortable, just open your eyes," I say.

It goes quiet—probably only for a few seconds. The balance between challenging and supporting is a delicate one. Learning and discovery of something new occurs some place between too much excitement and too much safety; I hope that we are there. I'm all eyes and ears, so alert and present that it's like I cross space and time and am sitting there beside her.

"Okay. Now you sense your feet on the floor, the support from the sofa, your breath. You can open your eyes again when you are ready."

Anna opens her eyes. What has she discovered? What more can she say about the hamster wheel?

"Is there anything that stands out that you wish to share and explore further?"

"I think the fear I initially felt is connected with me not being in control, when I entered the imaginary journey, and not knowing what would happen," she says.

Again a confirmation that the overarching experiment is always the relationship: to do an unfamiliar experiment and thus trust me was in itself significant for Anna, more than the instructions and the content of the guided fantasy itself. Here with me as well, the need for control arises. And this is linked to fear. I am a new man in her life. Anna is suspicious of men. At the same time, hopefully, she feels more confident about me, since I'm also her therapist. In any case, she is trying something new here and now with me. She enters into an unknown experiment, lets go of a little control, allows herself to be a little afraid.

"Do you recognise this need for control at other times in life?" I ask.

"Yes," she replies.

"And the opposite of control?"

"Hmm. In a way. Yes, I'm also adventurous. I live and work abroad, for example."

Adventurous, I wouldn't have guessed that that would be the counter-pole. So now we have two counter-poles to control thus far: sadness and adventurousness.

"I can recognise these sides in myself as well," I say, "and I recognise it in our relationship, how we do this together. We don't know each other so well yet, are not yet safe and intimate, so it's not strange that we try to control a lot. But daring to be in a relationship, perhaps especially in romantic relationships—but not limited to this sort—requires that we let go and open ourselves. Even therapy and other dialogue involve letting go and a sense of adventure. Even I, as the therapist, don't know where the session and the dialogue will go, what will emerge and which direction we will take, that this came out of the hamster wheel, for example."

"I guess the relationship with Dylan became a project that failed in so many ways," she says.

"Project," I repeat.

"Yeah, I think I saw it as one of my projects sometimes."

"Something that you had control over?"

"Yeah," she says, "and that is something that I recognise from my family. My mother and grandmother are also quite controlling. They received—and took—far too much responsibility in their relationships. I don't want to end up having that sort of relationship."

So control and responsibility—some sort of top dog perhaps—have been the women's role. A not uncommon adaptation following infidelity is to try to control the partner in order to prevent a new betrayal, or at least to expose it. Understandable enough. At the same time this often has a negative effect on the relationship. Infidelity is the quintessential power play, argue some family and couples therapists. When one partner feels that the other has taken too much control and power in the relationship and that they are not seen and respected, infidelity can be another adaptation. This is also understandable. Infidelity can trigger control; control can trigger infidelity. It's difficult to say what comes first. Both parties often play a part. Perhaps both can also contribute to change. Anna, in any case, doesn't want to only take the role of the partner who controls and takes responsibility. And with me she has already done something else, been a little adventurous in the experiment.

"Can you say *I want to have control and I want to be adventurous?*" I suggest.

"I want to have control and I want to be adventurous."

"How does that feel?" I ask.

"Natural. It fits me." Anna exhales. A little more whole already, I think, not simply one role.

"I think loving each other and ourselves, and achieving change, involves knowing and recognising the different sides of ourselves and the other," I say. "Then it also becomes possible to be whole and flexible, to move between these sides, depending on what the situation and the relationship requires here and now; sometimes control, other times adventurousness."

We begin to wrap up and agree to meet in her city for the next session, since I'm going to visit my partner who lives there.

We smile and shake hands. I show her into the flat of my partner, who is at work. Anna and I sit down in two armchairs in the living room.

"You know the guy I mentioned in our first session, the guy I went home with and then I saw all that girl stuff, and fled from the next morning?" she says.

I nod.

"A few days ago I suggested by text that we meet again," she continues. "He said that he couldn't. It was a very long and nice message, actually. He wanted to try again with his ex-girlfriend. I allowed myself to be sad, and tears came."

"So you let yourself be sad and cry," I say. "You had a new experience with this new man."

"Yeah. Even if he wasn't someone I knew well, to be the one who isn't chosen hurts. And then it was really nice, how this became a good closure in contrast to how it ended with Dylan."

"Yeah," I say. "Do you still also feel the need for more of a closure with Dylan?"

"Not to meet him physically or communicate with him."

"What if we imagine that we have him sitting on a chair here?" I ask. "Unlike last time, where the two sides of you communicated on the red sofa, you could communicate with your version of him, a projection of Dylan. It is after all your version of him that continues to haunt you and your new relationships with men."

"Let's try that," she says.

I stand up from the armchair and get two chairs from the kitchen. "You can place them however you want. In one you can be yourself, and in the other imagine Dylan."

Anna places the chairs facing each other. Looks at them. Adjusts the distance. Sits down. "I feel nervous. I wish that we had broken up earlier. I want to say that I forgive, but that isn't how I feel now."

I forgive, central in both religious and therapeutic traditions. But this is exactly why it can also be experienced as something one *should* do,

I think. It's important that Anna herself feels that she *can* and *wants* to. Then, forgiveness can involve letting go of something old and painful, a fixed gestalt can become less fixed. But often it is first necessary to really feel the painful emotions. Change happens when one becomes who one is.

"What are you feeling now?" I ask.

"I don't know."

It's quiet. Will she again try to control herself? Or will she express a counter-pole? Sadness? Adventurousness? Something else?

Anna begins to cry. I pull back a little. She sits facing an empty chair, Dylan. She cries for a little while. Then resolutely she dries her tears away. "I can't believe that you took away all the photos of us together. That was cruel."

Photos of us together? Won't she say something about the infidelity? I don't understand. But Anna understands. And now I hear anger in her voice; I can understand that this is important.

"If you want, you can also try to respond from his chair," I suggest after a while.

She moves to the other chair. "I didn't want you to have anything that reminded you of our life together," she says from there.

And I can understand that the photos are important. They represent their history together. She's been concerned with the fact that she has a history. And this history has not only been painful. They've probably also had some good memories together, and then he takes all of the photos and the entire history away from her.

She sits in her own chair **again**. "I hate you for that," she says.

Then it is quiet, for a long time, until she changes chairs. "I'm sorry. I hate myself for that as well."

She switches back, calmer in her movements now. "It's okay. Just don't ever do that to anyone else," she says.

Then comes a long exhale. Anna lets go; I believe she does. *It's okay, just don't ever do that to anyone else.* How far in time and space does this extend? Is she and her family out of the hamster wheel, freed from the curse?

"It's silent now," she says and looks at me.

"Just sit for a while in the silence. When you are ready, you can get up from the chair."

She gets up. We stand beside the chairs and look at them. That relationship is over, Dylan and Anna, just two empty chairs now.

"I wanted to forgive, one should forgive of course, but there and then I felt first sadness and then anger," she explains.

"Yeah," I say, "and then you were able to forgive afterwards, let go of him and what he had done."

"I think that I can forgive myself as well now. For what I did wrong, my contribution to everything, that my relationship with him became a project."

"I'm touched, Anna. Witnessing this has been beautiful. And I'm also touched because you have trusted me, opened up for these feelings and the unknown in this way with me here and now. I think that also means something."

Again a few tears. I sense some pressing from under my eyes too.

"Relief," she says.

"It feels as if I'm cleansed, like I've washed my entire body. Something is resolved." Anna smiles at me via Skype. "I'm happy. And I don't know what I should bring up in this session. I thought earlier this week that maybe I could talk more about my childhood. On the other hand, I feel we've already explored what was my main issue."

Something is resolved. A fixed gestalt has become less fixed. Anna has had new and perhaps transformational experiences with the man she met in the bar, with me, with the projection of Dylan. Anna is happy. Shall we go to her childhood? If nothing pressing comes up here and now, we can leave it be. It seems like this is mostly a preconception she has about therapy, about how one should be as a client, have something to offer me and preferably childhood trauma.

"You don't need to tell me about your childhood for my sake," I say.

How would it be to be together without anything and anyone between Anna and me now? Without the curse, without Dylan, without a history and a project, how would that be?

"We can be together with what is here and now. How does it feel to not have a plan, to not have anything to talk about, that something is resolved and that you are happy?"

"I don't know," she replies.

"We can see what happens; what we feel and want right here and now?"

It's quiet for a long time. Then she speaks. "I'm thinking about what we have accomplished. I've gotten so much out of our sessions. I think that the holistic approach to body, mind and soul has been very useful."

To summarise, remember and evaluate, that is what is happening now, I think. We are getting close to the end, I guess.

"I'm happy to hear that," I say. "I've experienced you as very motivated and dedicated to the process, Anna. You have a high degree of awareness and will to explore. All of this makes therapy more effective."

"Awareness. For some reason that word stuck with me now. I do yoga and meditation. Maybe I haven't mentioned that?" she says and tells me about her practice. I also tell her a little bit about my own.

"If you feel adventurous, the two of us could try a form of meditation together here and now?" I suggest and smile. "A relational meditation, where we see each other, listen, sense each other, and are aware of what is here and now between us and how it affects us."

"That sounds interesting."

I look at Anna and calmly move my gaze and let go of thoughts; I really see her and share my awareness with her.

"My gaze is moving. I see a little redness in your cheeks; your blonde hair down on one side of your head and your neck; that you are smiling now, something is happening with your eyes."

"And I feel a tingling in my stomach when you say that," she says.

It goes quiet for a moment.

"I wonder if you see me, Anna. Can you describe something that you see?"

"I see your shoulders now. I move my gaze more."

"I see that, and think that you see me better now as your gaze moves more. And that makes me happy," I say.

We continue like this for a while.

"Shall we talk a bit about what we have done?" I suggest.

"It was beautiful. I felt that you were very real to me. And that I was very real to you—and myself," she says.

"I experienced that as well," I say. "We often take a lot of the old along with us into relationships and situations. Sometimes it can overshadow what is novel and fresh. It can be helpful to remember that thoughts are thoughts, worries are worries, history is history, and to also be aware of what one actually hears, sees and can otherwise experience here and now with the new person in the new situation."

"That makes sense. I've carried many thoughts relating to Dylan and my family history with me into new relationships," she says. "I realised that I also carry with me a sort of mental checklist. In a way, I'm mentally sitting there and crossing off whether the other person fits certain predetermined criteria. I think that I'm going to put less emphasis on that list as well."

"Then perhaps you can more easily experience what isn't on the checklist or a part of the project or the plan, a little like we just did now together in meditation."

She nods and smiles.

During the next session, Anna confirms that there is nothing in particular she wants to address in therapy at the moment. We agree to end this round, but that she can contact me again any time. We spend much of the session summarising what we've done and learnt together. We finish with a new guided fantasy. The therapy is a journey we've travelled together, I think to myself, a path that becomes clearer as we walk.

"You and I are walking along a path in the forest. What is around you, and what do you sense inside yourself?" I ask. "Then, we pause somewhere and rest. From here you go onwards by yourself. How is this? What do you experience? What do you become aware of in yourself and around you?" I wait for a moment. "Now, when you are ready, you can again sense your breath, the contact with the floor and the sofa and open your eyes."

"It began in darkness, and I was a little afraid, but it felt safe walking together with you," she says. "When I went onwards alone, it was day and sunlight, and I was curious and noticed new things in the forest and was content."

There is motion this time, I think, change and motion like there has been in the therapy. She's no longer stuck in the hamster wheel.

"At some point I stopped by a tree. I picked an apple," she continues.

An apple, is this the Garden of Eden and the Tree of Knowledge? Talk about adventurousness. Are new curses in the making? I don't know. It's paradoxical how my thoughts land on the Tree of Knowledge, and at the same time I know that I cannot know what this means for her. So what does the apple mean to Anna?

"Does any of this make sense in your life now?" I ask.

"Yes, I feel that I'm ready to go onwards alone, curious and open," she replies. "The apple is a bit of a mystery to me. But I associate it with something that is ripe and within reach. And that there is motion and change in everything, like seeds that become trees that produce fruits that fall to the ground and so on."

So, this is our final image. The curse is broken, I believe it is.

Comments on "Three generations of betrayal"

Infidelity: Infidelity can be defined as situations where one party in an established relationship enters into an intimate, emotional and/or sexual relationship with a third person, without the other party's knowledge of and acceptance of this.[1] Some family and couples therapists believe that "infidelity is the quintessential power play" (Wedge, 2013, unpaginated), that it can be linked to an experience of not feeling seen, heard and respected in a relationship. In Norwegian and American surveys roughly 30 to 70 per cent of men report being unfaithful.[2] As a rule, it is less common for women, but the gender difference has been closing over the years. Studies show that the one who is deceived can experience a lost sense of control and predictability and a need to regain this, and experience reactions that are similar to post-traumatic stress, depression, and other conditions. The one who is or has been unfaithful can also have similar experiences.[3]

Trauma and post-traumatic stress: Whereas people once associated trauma with rare and extreme events, there is now an increased understanding that even common, stressful events such as traffic accidents, as well as long-term processes such as bullying, can be traumas and result in post-traumatic stress disorder.[4] A sense of helplessness generally increases the risk of developing post-traumatic stress disorder.[5]

Post-traumatic stress disorder can manifest in various ways:[6] Flashbacks are an experience of reliving the traumatic event as if it is happening now. Many people try to avoid talking about or thinking about what happened, and avoid people or places that remind them of the event. One can feel excited, tense, nervous, irritable, and angry. Many also have symptoms such as dizziness, nausea, headaches, and a feeling that their heart is beating very fast or hard.

After the Second World War, professor in psychiatry and neuroscience Rachel Yehuda and other researchers conducted a number of studies that explored the traumatisation of Holocaust survivors and their children.[7] One thing they found was that children of survivors can be more vulnerable than others to stress and trauma. Something is transmitted. Research now indicates that strong emotional experiences can alter the expression of genes.[8] A disposition can thereafter be inherited. At the same time, this means that another type of emotional experience can change things for a person here and now as well as for future generations. In other words, wounds can heal and curses can be broken.

Support and challenge: To support and to challenge can be seen as two sides of a polarity. Gestalt therapy has also experienced a polarisation of these sides, including between Laura and Fritz Perls. It may be that I—and many other current gestalt therapists—now experience a (too strong?) shift towards support, following a period where Fritz Perls and challenge and confrontation were more dominant. An integration of the polarity in gestalt therapists and the therapy is also important. According to professor in psychology and pedagogics Nevitt Sanford, learning and growth occur when a proper balance between support and challenge is struck, and the person is ready for the change.[9] What constitutes the proper balance depends upon the particular person and the situation here and now.

Forgiveness: To let go of painful feelings and thoughts about another person who has done something wrong generally requires that you first become aware of these feelings and thoughts—for example, sadness and anger in Anna's case—and work through them. Forgiveness can then be a way of finishing something unfinished from the past. Such an approach is consistent with gestalt therapy.[10] Studies have shown the effectiveness of forgiveness in cases of infidelity and the connections between forgiveness in general and a long list of positive health effects, such as reducing stress, depression, anxiety, and post-traumatic reactions.[11]

Effective therapy: Many researchers find that therapy in general is relatively effective regardless of the particular school or method—whether it is cognitive therapy, psychoanalysis, gestalt therapy, or something else—and there are certain common factors in all therapy that make it effective.[12] Among the common factors are the client's and therapist's motivation, faith in the theory and method they use, and good cooperation, where the client is able to give feedback and the therapist takes this feedback into account. In other words, people and relationships matter more than specific techniques.

CHAPTER FOUR

Marianne's memories

Marianne is crying. It's our second session together. She sits before me and cries and cries. *Abuse.* Words from our first session come to mind. *It has to do with abuse.* I don't know anything more. Now I hear only crying and see only her red hair and hands covering her face. Where is she really? Does she disappear into the tears, into a flashback from the assault, the past experienced as though it is the present? Am I losing her now? What should I do? My stomach tenses. I hold my breath. Yet at the same time, as I become aware of this, I can draw a deep breath and exhale calmly. I feel my back, rear and thighs against the chair. My feet on the floor. I am here. Calmer. Now I can also invite her to feel a foundation while she cries.

"Can you feel the chair and the ground while you cry, Marianne?"

"No," she says, but calms down a little nonetheless. "Maybe we can sit on the floor?"

"Yes," I say. "It's great that you know how to support yourself and ask for support."

Therapy is meant to be a collaboration, not advice and guidance from an expert high above the helpless, not abuse. We push the chairs away and sit down on the tile floor. I give her a pillow and take one myself. This is our common foundation.

Marianne begins to cry again, but more calmly. Occasionally I glance over at her: face in her hands, back hunched over, turned inwardly into herself. Suddenly I feel quite alone. Maybe she does too. Maybe that is a common element in all suffering, the experience of being alone. Yet, I am sitting together with her now and sense that I am being affected. How can she more clearly experience that we are together? Perhaps I could sit a little closer to her? Careful, I think. *It has to do with abuse.*

"Is it okay if I sit a little closer beside you?" I ask.

She nods slightly, and I sit down beside her.

"Just cry, Marianne, but let me be with you."

I sense and hear that I exhale. Maybe she notices as well. Exhaling calms the nervous system. I sense it. Maybe it calms more than my system alone. People can affect each other spontaneously and bodily. This could mean that if I become aware of my breathing, she can also become aware of her own. So tight is the connection between us. Maybe I can breathe a little for the both of us. We sit like this for a while. A sort of confluence, this way of being together, a flowing together. I hear that she exhales, and it is calmer.

"I'm going to move back to my corner so I can sit facing you and see you more clearly again," I say.

Marianne looks up. A small crucifix hangs from a necklace around her neck.

"I've received a letter regarding compensation. They used a word for what I've experienced. It was retraumatising," she says. Her gaze again erratic. It's about trauma, about wounds. She has already cried a lot here, and I have let her. But we don't yet know each other very well. We are not entirely safe. At the same time, I don't want her to feel rejected.

"I'm listening and willing to hear you tell me more about this, Marianne. At the same time, I want you to be aware that you are sharing something with me now, and that you consider how much you want to tell me here and now."

"Yes, I've been considering this all week. I want to tell you. I guess I'd told them that I'd been taken to a place where there were other people. My uncle and his friends. The lawyers used the word *gang rape*. I think that was the last time. I was thirteen."

My God. *Uncle. Gang rape.* My stomach tenses. *I think that was the last time. I was thirteen.* I breathe again. Feel the floor. A blanket is hanging on one of the chairs. I can give her the blanket so that she can choose to cover herself a little, protect herself, while she opens up and talks about the abuse. Maybe it will protect me as well.

"I got an impulse to give you this blanket." I stand up and get the blanket. "If you want it?"

Marianne smiles and takes the blanket. She spreads it across her chest, stomach, lap and thighs as she sits on the floor. Now this can be clearly experienced as something new, different from back then, I think. This is not abuse. She can cover herself and open up at the same time. She can choose.

"I got pregnant, but lost the baby after a few months. No one knew about it. It was a double sorrow, because it was a child of incest that shouldn't have been born, but just the same it was a baby."

"Yes," I say.

"It is as though a light switch is turned on and off, and I see just glimpses of what happened. I disassociated while it happened. It was a good adaptation then, but not so anymore."

Marianne uses these kinds of words, *disassociated, adaptation*. During our first session, she told me that she already had a long history with psychiatry and therapy. Her adaptation to a situation where she couldn't fight or flee was to freeze and cut off what she sensed and felt in and through her body, to mentally disappear from what was happening. Good that she can see that it was a good adaptation then, and that she is not ashamed of it. And at the same time, she sees that it isn't always so helpful anymore.

"How is it right now when you are sharing this with me?" I ask.

"I don't sense my body, only from my neck up," she says.

A reaction that certainly resembles disassociation. And not uncommon after traumatisation. Still, maybe we can try something new here and now. Maybe I can guide her awareness towards sense impressions of me. Maybe she can experience that this is a different situation and relationship, that what she is talking about are memories and not something happening here and now.

"Do you see me? Can you describe what you see?" I ask.

"You are wearing a green shirt, blue jeans," she replies.

"Do you see my face as well? Can you describe it?"

"You have a beard."

So she can be present with her senses in this situation. Our session is coming to an end. We have looked a little closer at a wound. The image that comes to mind is that we put on a bandage and conclude for now.

"We have opened up for something. Do you know how you can close for now? How do you usually close? And how can we do this together here?" I ask.

"I've tried mindfulness. It helps sometimes," she replies.

"So you can close as well as open. That's good," I say. "Mindfulness and sensing here and now can be good approaches to dealing with trauma. We also do this in gestalt therapy. We have already done it a little by focusing on what you can sense here and now together with me. Maybe this is a good enough conclusion for today."

"After finishing, he would just leave. But often a reward would come shortly afterwards." Suddenly she cries again. "I'm a whore."

Like a blow to the stomach. *I'm a whore*. We need to conclude now, but how? How can I do this without it being brutal, without me being yet another person who simply leaves after we have opened something? Perhaps I can recognise this ambivalence, at least.

"I understand that this is important, Marianne, and at the same time we need to wrap up our session. I want us to find a way to temporarily close this together."

She cries and cries. She clearly doesn't want to close, doesn't want to or simply can't. It's flowing over.

"We need to conclude now, Marianne. But it seems you find it difficult. Am I right?"

"Yes. I am going straight to my office afterwards, and they don't know anything," she says. "Next time, I want to have a more open day, maybe go to a café and write a little in order to land after the session."

"So you write as well. Then we have a common interest." I want to build an alliance and a relationship, an experience of community and cooperation. And with this subject we are perhaps on less disturbing ground, I think to myself, perhaps making it easier to conclude.

"I've spent a lot of my childhood in books. That has helped," she says.

"That's good. Therapy can also be a story that we create together."

I guess the session is continuing after all. Yet, we must close. Suddenly an image comes to mind: we light a candle together. Where did that come from? Maybe because she said that it was like a light switch being turned off and on when she remembered the abuse. Maybe due to the little crucifix hanging around her neck. Light can symbolise hope, I think to myself, that even if we close and conclude now, we can continue next time. That even though she has experienced something terrible in the past, there is a future. I don't know where it came from, but I trust the image.

"I've got an idea. Let's light a candle together as a way of closing. And this candle will be here when you come next time as well. We can continue together later."

"Yes!" She looks at me and smiles.

We stand up. I give her a lighter, and she lights a red candle on the table. We stand beside one another. Again simply this being together. We are quiet as though in a church, and look at the small flame for a few seconds.

When Marianne has left, I blow out the candle, and everything becomes a little darker. I leave the therapy room and close the door, but I still feel something in my body. It isn't completely closed or concluded. Of course not. Of course I'm affected. These are atrocious abuses, abuses that far too many children experience and that far too often involve family members and other caregivers. I sense something bodily, indeterminable, a vague sense of a foundation that has become more fragile. I lie down on the sofa. I'm held by something other than myself. I need this.

I clear away the chairs and lay out pillows and a blanket on the floor so that it's ready when Marianne arrives. Now the tree outside has yellow leaves that shine in the autumn sun. I smile. When the doorbell rings, I take a moment, breathe, and feel the floor under my feet before I open.

"How nice. You're starting to know me." She smiles when she sees the pillows and blanket on the floor in the therapy room. We sit down, and she wraps the blanket around her shoulders.

"There's an image that has appeared repeatedly over the last few nights, some sort of dream. I know that it's a cemetery, but it's very unclear. I'm curious about it."

"We can enter the image and explore it further if you wish, see what emerges here and now, see if we can fill in the image a bit more," I suggest.

"Okay."

"Then you can close your eyes and go to the image here and now."

Marianne closes her eyes. I do so as well. This is becoming more common. I have to remember to not completely flow together with her.

"Are you in the cemetery now? What do you see around you? What do you feel?" I ask.

"There are rows of plain, white crosses. A large wall in the background."

"Maybe you hear or smell something?"

"Soil. Autumn. I stand still. And this is where it stops."

"Okay. Let's say that you now can actively continue dreaming. In a dream, everything is possible. Simply allow it to unfold. Remain where you are and see what you want to do, what you do, or what is happening here and now. We have time."

"I'm walking along the crosses. I stop beside one. There's nothing written on it. I write *my little angel* in grey. And then I lay down some white flowers. There is a faint fragrance, no strong smells or colours."

I'm following along with her. I'm feeling along with her. Occasionally, I open my eyes slightly to see and check how things are going. She's crying a little, but I think that we're okay.

"Now I light a candle. I can cry uninhibited, since there's nobody else here. But I also know that I have to go back to my life. I just want to say a prayer first."

She goes quiet. I also pray a silent prayer—for Marianne, to whom or what I don't know. But I know that it affects me, strengthens my motivation and wishes for her well-being. And so, I assume, it will also somehow affect her in relation with me.

"Now I walk back to where I began," she says.

"Okay. Let's slowly come out of the image now. Feel the ground beneath you and your breath. You can slowly open your eyes and return to this room."

Marianne opens her eyes. Her gaze is steady, her breathing calm. She looks at me. We talk a little about what she experienced.

"It feels good to have my own place to go in the image, some sort of grave. It was actually this time of year when the baby died," she says.

"So she died in the autumn. Now I said *she*. For some reason I imagined the child as a girl, but you haven't said anything about that."

"No," she replies, "I don't know of course, but I also imagined that it was a girl."

Where does reality stop? Where does imagination and fantasy begin? This was an image from a dream, and we have continued to live it through imagination.

"There were many psychiatrists who didn't believe me. They didn't believe that there had actually been abuse or a child. Several have suggested that I should see a doctor to confirm whether I have ever been pregnant or not. I haven't. I guess I don't want to know with certainty."

Of course there is no grave. Was there a child? Was there abuse? The lawyers believed her. There were several psychiatrists that didn't believe her. Do I believe her? I think so. Why wouldn't I? Yet why doesn't she just go to a doctor and confirm the pregnancy like the psychiatrists suggested? She would rather not know with certainty, she says. Maybe it would hurt too much.

"I went around in a state of constant preparedness right until my uncle died. That was when I was twenty," she continues. "As I said, the last abuse happened when I was thirteen. But there are subtle ways of keeping a person down, with the occasional touch, a glance, or a comment. It was only after he died that I began to remember. The flashbacks came. And then it was straight into psychiatry."

Now she is almost forty. She said so during the first session. So all of this is from some time ago. And she also has a good imagination. That became clear from the guided fantasy around the image from the cemetery. Not that Marianne is inventing stories intentionally, but the past exists as memories here and now, memories that change, not entirely unlike how we continued the imagination of the scene from the cemetery. *False memories do occur.* Didn't I just read this in an article on sexual abuse? *Memory changes with time.* Maybe I'll have a moment to take a look at that again before the next client.

"We often went to his grave and placed flowers there and expressed how much we missed him and talked about good memories. Sometimes I thought that perhaps it never really happened, or that it wasn't so bad, that maybe I remembered incorrectly, maybe I never had that child."

"You also doubt yourself sometimes," I say.

"Yes. I need to protect myself with that doubt sometimes. That maybe it never actually happened."

A way of surviving, I guess, to allow herself to doubt sometimes as well.

"How did it feel to give all this some space with me here now?" I ask.

"It felt good. It was nice to not feel judged," she replies.

"I'm touched, Marianne. Judging you is the last thing I want to do."

We begin to close, stand up, and light the candle.

After the session my gaze falls upon a collection of Freud's texts on the bookshelf. Certainly, no one has been more occupied with children and sexuality than him. I read a little from the story about Dora. First, he believed her and other patients when they talked about abuse that they had experienced in their childhood, but after a while he started to mainly interpret these as sexual fantasies. The first gestalt therapists were also originally psychoanalysts. They certainly understood sex in a different way, but they didn't really recognise abuse either. Fortunately, some development has taken place. Yet, even today, there are many psychiatrists, psychologists and therapists who talk about false memories. Contributing to the creation of new or strengthening of old false memories of abuse is something I certainly don't want to do. On the other hand, meeting someone with an abuse story with doubt and alternate interpretations, no, that seems almost as cruel. Also a form of abuse. Fortunately, Marianne felt the session went well. She said so. I didn't judge her. Still, doubt and belief are undeniably phenomena emerging between the two of us in the therapy room.

The doorbell rings, and I'm thrown out of my thoughts. Next client. I place Freud back on the bookshelf.

I'm reading an article on narrative exposure therapy. Maybe I can use some of this with Marianne. I spend a lot of time on her—outside of our sessions as well. I look outside. The leaves are falling from the tree. Soon only a dark skeleton will remain. I receive a text message:

> I'm struggling like hell. But I'm fighting to come and see you. Violent flashbacks. Broke down over a garbage can. I'm in pain. Marianne.

I call, but she doesn't pick up. I send a text message back:

> Hi Marianne! If you don't come to me, I can come to you somewhere. Just send a message or call. Otherwise I'll see you here. We'll do this together.

I receive a new text message:

> I'm slowly moving, in the right direction.

I read a little more in the article. After a while, the bell rings. Her hair is a mess. Eyes wide open. She takes off her jacket and quickly goes into the therapy room.

"It has to do with the first rape," she begins, her gaze to floor.

It seems like she feels the need to tell me this, to share these stories. Yet, is this healing for her, to open up in this way? And what about me, what do I feel? Compassion. Yes, a lot of compassion for her. Still, there is something else as well. I think that I'm often overwhelmed together with Marianne. I breathe again. I feel the floor beneath me. Warmth. There are heating cables under the stone tiles, and I have turned up the temperature now that autumn is here and we sit on the floor. *The lifeline*, I think. I can suggest an approach that resembles the one I just read about in the article.

"I have a suggestion, Marianne. If you want to tell me more, we can imagine that one of these lines on the floor is your lifeline. On this line we find your birth, good and bad memories, the first rape, and here where you are now together with me."

"That sounds interesting," she says.

"When we experience danger or crisis, it's often the case that certain sense impressions are strong and remembered well, while others are weak and we are less aware of them," I explain. "As you yourself have said, disassociation may have been a good adaptation there and then. Part of the reasoning behind the approach I'm suggesting is to become more aware of and put into words what is less conscious but still in the body. This is why while you speak, I will ask about what you sensed inside your body, sense impressions from the outside, what you felt, and what you thought. Maybe the memories will become clearer and integrated, maybe transformed, into the larger story of yourself, into a new story that you're telling in a safe environment here and now with me."

Marianne nods.

"Okay. First, you can choose a line and mark your birth somewhere on it."

"Here," she says and runs her finger along a line that goes between us. "And here is my birth," she says, letting her finger rest just in front of her.

"And where you are now in life?" I ask.

She points at a place closer to me.

"And the first rape?"

She points at a place on the line, just a few centimetres after her birth.

"I suggest that you begin to tell me about a memory prior to this. A good one, perhaps?" I say.

"I'm in preschool." She points at another place on the lifeline.

"Okay. What do you see? What do you hear? Are you with anyone? What are you doing?" I ask.

"We're playing. My little sister is also here. But she wants to go home to mom. She begins to cry and goes towards the gate. But I go to her, and she comes back with me to the sandbox. We continue playing." Marianne smiles. "There is so much I remember once we get started."

"So this is a good memory. You sense it in your body now. You're smiling," I point out.

"Yes."

We let the good memory sink in for a moment.

"Okay. Now let's go to the first rape," I say. "I want you to begin the story a little while before the actual incident. Use as many of your senses as possible."

"It was summer, the summer before I was to start school, the summer my mother got sick and we spent a lot of time at my uncle's," she says.

"Where exactly are you now in that memory? Do you sense anything?"

"I'm outside in their garden, on the gravel and the grass, in the sun. My uncle comes out and says that he wants to take me to a nearby farm. We go hand in hand."

"How do you feel?"

"I'm happy. We go over to a field, stopping from time to time, and he tells me about some flowers. Eventually we come to a barn."

"What do you see? What do you smell and hear?"

"It's dim, there's a pungent smell of animals and hay, lots of yellow hay. It's quiet. I want to jump in the hay, but he holds my hand tight."

I'm asking questions in present tense, and she's replying in present tense. Should we do that? Will this become too intense? What did it say in that article? I'll have to think about this later. I can't stop now.

"He pushes me down onto the hay."

"What do you sense? What do you feel and think?"

"I feel something poking my back, the hay. I want to get away. He holds my shoulder with one hand, pulls my panties down, and opens the zipper on his grey pants. Then I disappear from my body." She looks at me.

"Okay. What happens next? You disappear from your body. Even so, see if you now can recall any sensations, feelings, sense impressions. We have time and you are safe here."

"He forces himself inside of me. Terrible pain. He moves back and forth against me like a wave. Then he gets up and goes to the door. I look down, blood everywhere. I'm afraid that I'll die. I need to hide this, I think to myself, because nobody will believe me. No one would believe this about my kind uncle."

I cast a glance at the clock. Only five minutes left. Still, we can't stop here. We need to move along the lifeline to a somewhat safer place.

"What happens next?" I ask.

"Slowly I get up, collect my clothes, and go to the door. It's warmer and lighter outside. I walk along a tractor road back to the house. Nobody is there. I find clean underwear and go into the bathroom. The smell of an old bathroom. I try to wash myself, but it hurts. Then I see that it wasn't so much blood after all. I put the old underwear at the bottom of the garbage bag. Then I go out to the garden again."

"What do you sense there?"

"Grass and gravel. The sun is shining. And then I hear my little sister's voice in the distance. I'm glad that she is okay."

"I think that we will stop here for now, Marianne. We will stop with you out on the grass, in the sun, hearing your little sister's voice and being glad that she is okay. How do you feel now after telling me about this?"

"I have of course told this to others, but not in such detail. What do you think after hearing it?"

"Is there anything in particular that you want to know?"

"Do you believe the story?"

What can I say? I don't know. Still, I must answer, and I don't want to lie.

"I've followed you in your descriptions, imagined the yellow hay, and all that happened."

"It's important to me. Otherwise our dialogue would have shipwrecked. I've been to therapists who didn't believe me."

Otherwise our dialogue would have shipwrecked. A boat, that is the metaphor for our dialogue, a boat on a vast and open ocean, I think. *He moves back and forth against me like a wave,* Marianne said about the rape. We need to take good care of this boat.

"Yes, I understand. What about you?" I ask.

"Sometimes I believe it, other times I don't."

"Yes."

"Do you see me differently now? Do you think that I was partly to blame?" she asks.

"No, you were a child."

"I didn't resist."

"To a large extent, it's an instinctive part of us that decides the most appropriate reaction to danger. You were a child. It may not have helped to try to escape or resist."

"I feel ashamed," she says.

A pressure in my chest. It's terrible that she's the one who feels ashamed. It's also so typical, that it's the person who has experienced the abuse who feels shame. I want to give some space for the shame, that at least she needn't be ashamed of the shame. On the other hand, we have gone way past our allotted time already.

"It's good that you can identify the feeling of shame, Marianne. But now we must begin to close. We'll meet again for new sessions and can explore this more."

"I'm a whore."

"I hear that you say you're a whore. And I don't think that way about you."

"It feels like I'm still there where it happened, like I'm a child."

I point at a place on the tile floor. "That was there." Then I point at the place closer to me. "And here you are now. We have more information about the first rape. You've described yellow hay, a pungent smell of animals and many other sense impressions from that time. Here it is different. Here and now it is not the same. Here you are sitting with me on this floor in this room." I stand up. "Let's light the candle."

She gets up. Reluctant, but obedient, I think. This is horrible. Yet we must close now. We must. I light the candle. We stand beside one another, together, but it doesn't feel good.

The next day I receive an email from Marianne:

> I experienced the last session as upsetting. In retrospect I maybe could have stopped. But at the same time I slid into a state where I just answered your questions. I entered a state where I pretty much could have done anything. This is, unfortunately, all too familiar. I do as I'm told. I don't complain. It wasn't so bad yesterday. But even so I am left with a feeling of having said too much. Not because I think that you can't handle it, but because I feel that it wasn't right for me. This is an experience we can take with us in the future. See you next Monday.

I'm retraumatising her, I think to myself. It feels as though something breaks in my chest, like something collapses inside of me. What kind of therapist am I? Several years of training as a gestalt therapist in how to be aware of what is happening between us and I simply push on and slavishly follow a technical approach. I asked and she replied—we flowed together in a destructive manner, one that coincided with the rape itself. The waves. The blood. Maybe not exactly abuse, but this too has to do with boundaries. Shame. Yes, it's shame I now feel.

Okay, Vikram, breathe, I say to myself. I can also make mistakes. I have learnt something from this. Don't lose sight of the relationship. Don't become too caught up in techniques such as the lifeline and others, regardless of how safe it may feel to cling to these. Now that it has happened, this can also be a therapeutic opportunity. Her email is proof that in the end she did in fact protest. I write a reply:

> Thank you for writing so honestly to me, Marianne. In a way you are protesting now. And I want to apologise. I apologise that I was not more aware of your need for support to regulate opening and sharing on the one hand and closing and stopping on the other. I'm sorry that I ended while you still felt unsafe. From your email I understand that you want to stay. I will also stay and support you in your process. And I believe that this honesty, protest and staying are important parts of what we are exploring and doing together.

I receive a new email:

> Thanks for the nice reply.

"How is it going with you now, Marianne?" I ask the next time we meet. "We have been emailing, but I'd also like to check what you're feeling here and now. Is there anything else or more you wish to express?"

"I had some closure after that email," she replies. "It helped that you were so specific and clear, that it's okay for me to protest, that we can explore this further together, that there is space and time for this."

So it led to something good after all, I think. We've made an important experience together. In contrast to the first rape, Marianne now experienced that she could protest and be respected. In contrast to when she was a child, she could now resist—or flee if necessary. Maybe awareness of her needs and expressing protest can come slightly sooner as well—while we are sitting together face to face. I look at her.

"Can you say no to me when I suggest an experiment or during an experiment?" I ask.

"Both yes and no," she replies.

She is honest, I think, doesn't simply answer what she thinks I want to hear.

"Okay. Maybe we can try to be extra aware of that in the future. It can be more important to feel what you want than to complete an experiment and the particulars of an experiment."

She nods. Then she looks down at the floor and runs her finger along the line. "I became quite fascinated by the lifeline. I hope the integration of the memory works. In its wake some good memories also emerged. Some memories from my first day at school."

Wake. Again our dialogue as a boat. I like this image. The boat has not shipwrecked, and in its wake something good has also surfaced.

"Do you want to explore them with me now?" I ask.

"Yes."

"Where on the line are we?"

She points at a place on the line, after the first rape. "I'm together with my mom in the schoolyard."

"Good. Take your time. What do you see? What do you sense? What do you feel and think now?"

"The sun is shining. I'm excited. A flag is raised. I'm wearing green and purple clothes and a blue backpack. My mom had let me choose the clothes myself. The teacher is calling out our names. There are many children. Everyone equal somehow, everyone excited, everyone safe. It's some sort of new start."

"So this is a good episode on your lifeline, in the story of yourself."

"Yes. I'm also curious about what happens further down this line, in the future."

We get up and light the candle.

Afterwards I follow her to the foyer. She puts on her jacket. "Now I'm off to a café to write a little. I think that I'll write down the memory from my first day at school as well."

Marianne has made this into a routine, going down to the café on the corner and writing after our sessions. As with all of my clients, I also write notes in my journal following the sessions. One day we talk about these texts that each of us are writing. These are also stories. We could exchange a few texts and then talk about them. Perhaps I would get to know more about what Marianne is thinking and feeling, what she sees as important and effective in therapy and what can be improved. Maybe the things I have written down and my theoretical reflections may give her something more than what I have communicated during the sessions. Maybe reading about the sessions can give us both some perspectives and help us evaluate the therapy's course thus far. And last, but not least, it can be an experiment. We clarify what is here and now, our shared story, and see what happens. We agree to exchange texts.

A few days later I take a look at what I've written. Should I read through and edit it? No, it should be honest. Is there anything I have written that I wouldn't be able to share with her during the sessions? Maybe my doubts at times. Do I dare now? I edit just a little, save, upload, and press send. Soon I receive an email with Marianne's text. Then a little while later I get another email:

> I'm reading about your doubt. And I'm not completely sure what I should write. False memories are a reoccurring topic with mental health professionals. I've met with it before—and will surely meet it again.

Soon after I receive yet another email:

> No, actually this makes me angry. Really angry. If you don't believe me, we don't have anything further to build upon. I don't accept this.

I'm a failed therapist and, more importantly, a failed human being. This is my first thought. Shame. I shared too much and too quickly, again a lack of boundaries. Had I taken a sufficient look at the doubt in myself, explored it properly, before I shared this with her? I need to respond quickly. No, I should wait a little. Hold back. I contact my supervisor.

I meet him and tell him about Marianne and me. When I recount Marianne's story, he makes me aware that my eyes are wide-open, I exhale heavily; I show how unfathomable this is. Yes, it is unfathomable. Some people have experienced such terrible things that it is difficult to believe, painful to believe, difficult to accept. Then I also feel some sort of sadness, a sort of a global sadness in my entire body. He supports me and asks me to stay with that feeling. We are together, he is simply here with me, and he is not judging me. I feel supported by him. Maybe doubt has also been necessary for me from time to time, as it was for Marianne. If I truly take in this horror, am really shaken by it, what would happen then? I allow a few silent tears now, in the presence of my supervisor.

I send an email where I again apologise and try to convey some of this to Marianne. She replies that she will come to our next session. Back in the therapy room, I look at Freud's texts on the bookshelf. Maybe he and other therapists then as well as now experienced something similar. It is easier and safer with doubt and interpretations and techniques when confronted with horror.

"I have never protested so much in any therapeutic relationship, perhaps any relationship for that matter," Marianne says when we meet. "Thanks."

We smile. She has also understood that these are new and important experiences, her protesting and me apologising. And her protests were probably possible because we had built a good enough relationship. The boat floats. Yes, I am not entirely hopeless as a therapist and human being.

"The fact that you doubted also made me no longer doubt," she continues. "I felt more strongly than ever that I believe my own story."

I get some ideas about polarities, how doubt and belief play out within each of us and between us. But before I am able to think any further, I see that Marianne has begun to cry. She cries and cries; the kind of crying that comes from the stomach and shakes the entire body. I think about something she wrote in her text about the therapy. *And I think about your words: "Just cry, Marianne, but let me be with you". Thanks. That makes me less ashamed and alone.*

"Is it okay if I sit down beside you?" I ask.

She nods, and I move closer to her.

"He got off so easily, without ever being confronted," she says.

"Yes. When I listen to you, I also get very sad and angry." I hear that my voice trembles and falters while I speak, and I let it tremble and let it falter. I think we both believe the story now. Again we flow together, in a good way.

I think about something else from her text: *Maybe I'll dare to ask you to hold my hand one day, just a moment, a little while, know that I am not entirely alone.* Should I do it? Do I want to? I don't know. Again a question of boundaries and regulation. What is really okay for her, and what is okay for me? I check in with myself. No, not holding hands, but maybe a hand on the shoulder.

"Can I put a hand on your shoulder?" I ask.

"Yes," she replies while she continues to cry. I carefully put one hand on her shoulder.

"Do you feel my hand there?"

"Yes."

Here and now together with me she feels bodily sensations. This is a safe touch. The right amount of confluence, and the right amount of differentiation. Soon she stops crying, and I hear her exhale.

We sit like this for a while. We breathe. Then I move back to my corner.

She glances up, looks at me. "I'm also a little curious about what you think about my text."

"It was very interesting reading," I say. "Clients often highlight something other than what therapists believe to be important in therapy. But I think that we both agreed that the relationship was crucial. And I must also say that I think you write very well. I'm grateful that you let me read that text. At the end you wrote something about books and writing having been your salvation, that maybe one day your experiences and your story might help others. I hope and believe so too."

We light the candle.

Marianne and I meet throughout the winter. Now that there is less doubt, other phenomena begin to appear and become more clear and strong. I have problems breathing, and tensions in my body. During the night I find myself sleepless more and more due to nightmares, where I am not sure whether I am the abuser or the abused or perhaps both. Vicarious traumatisation, I think to myself. Now that my doubt is less present, I need to find other ways to regulate distance and closeness, our flow and our boundaries. I continue to meet my supervisor regularly. I decide to spend less time on Marianne between sessions. Yet what about her text messages and emails? I think that it has been good for her to have a safe relationship, to have a person who has also been available between sessions. Nevertheless, right now I can't bear it, and we are after all in another phase of the therapy where it is perhaps less necessary. Yet how can I say anything about this without her feeling rejected? She is unsure whether or not she can say no to me; can I say no to her? Marianne has good days and bad days throughout the winter. On one of the good days I find the courage.

"I think it has been appropriate that we have had a lot of contact for a period by email and text messages outside of our sessions, but now we are in a new phase, and I notice that it is too much for me. In the future, I want us to limit the contact to our sessions. If you later find it necessary to do so, we can make a new agreement. What do you think about that?"

"That's okay."

"How was it for you, me saying this? What do you feel now?"

"I'm glad that you are clear about what you need. Then I don't have to guess."

That went okay. Is it really okay? Is she honest? I choose to accept what she says. We create boundaries together. It's important for her to see that I am also clear about my needs.

Marianne smiles at me. Our eyes meet. I sense that I too smile. They're contagious, smiles. How tightly connected we humans are. I also notice that there is friendliness in the smile. Then I see a light falling on Marianne's cheek. She turns and looks out the window. The sun is shining. The tree has just begun to bud.

"What a beautiful tree," she says. "I haven't seen it until now."

"That's no small change. We both see the tree outside budding in the sunshine," I say.

"Yes."

We sit facing the sun and the tree for a moment. Calm sea, I think to myself.

"There has been another change as well," she says. I look at her. She turns and looks at me. "I stood in front of the mirror one day last week. And then suddenly I said to myself out loud: *You're actually okay.*"

* * *

Comments on "Marianne's memories"

Sexual abuse: According to a longitudinal study published in 2014 every third woman and every tenth man in Norway has experienced sexual abuse—every fifth woman before they've turned eighteen years old.[1] In addition, many have experienced different types of abuse and the majority of the known perpetrators were men. Few of those who experience abuse report it, tell others about it, or seek out health services. People who have experienced abuse generally have poorer mental health than others, including more anxiety, depression, and post-traumatic reactions.[2]

Fundamentally alone or connected: Many existentialists, including some gestalt therapists, consider isolation or loneliness—that we are fundamentally alone—as a basic condition in life. I emphasise Martin Buber's dialogical philosophy and other gestalt theories that posit that everyone and everything is tightly connected. Buber was himself critical to be being called an existentialist precisely because of many existentialists' belief that isolation/loneliness is a basic human condition. He writes, "There is no *I* taken in itself, but only the *I* of the primary word *I-Thou* and the *I* of the primary word *I-It*" (Buber, 2010, p. 4). Recent research, not least on mirror neurons as well as much infant research, supports this. The ability to relate to others and intersubjectivity are there from the start.[3]

At the same time, many people feel very alone at times. Maybe this is also the core of much suffering, that we feel that we are completely alone with what hurts. Perhaps this is also something that is partially linked to our time's focus on the individual. As a gestalt therapist I am interested in the client's subjective truth. By respecting and leaning into their reality an experience of community and connection can also emerge. This was clear in "Marianne's memories". One can also become aware that the experience of loneliness is something we all sometimes experience and share, thereby making it less lonely.

Furthermore, we must distinguish solitude as somewhat different from loneliness. Choosing to spend time by oneself can be very valuable and joyful. Spending time by oneself and being together with others can be seen as a polarity, and both poles can be beneficial.

Confluence: The word literally means "flowing together". It is also used specifically for places where two rivers join together and become one.

Sometimes this image is an appropriate description of my contact with Marianne. In addition, boat and sea became important images and metaphors. Our dialogue is a boat. "To be in the same boat" is also a well-known metaphor in our culture. It suggests an experience of community and of being dependent on one another. That we share a boat points to a confluence with greater opportunity for counter-poles like differentiation, than two rivers that completely merge into one.

There are other contact styles that I become aware of together with Marianne: projection of her uncle and previous experiences is something that occurs between us, and I am hoping for her to also experience me as different from this projection and our situation as a new situation. We share much, at times too much. The sharing and the expressiveness can also resemble confluence: it flows over, or we flow completely together. Perhaps retroflection also becomes a counter-pole to confluence in our relationship. As a whole, much of our work focused on striking a balance between aware confluence and aware differentiation and other counter-poles.[4]

The gestalt therapist Frank Staemmler relates confluence to empathy and highlights numerous healing qualities.[5] Among other things, empathy does something with the experience of being alone that is involved in almost all suffering. Even so-called "ruptures" in therapy can provide important therapeutic opportunities. Talking about what has happened in an empathetic way can repair, give hope that future situations can be dealt with, and contribute to developing skills to handle relationship crises. Marianne and I experience this when using the lifeline and after exchanging texts. She experiences that she is less alone, and eventually it is also clear that she has internalised a more empathetic relationship to herself. Generally speaking, a number of common factors of effective therapy can be seen as elements related to confluence and empathy.[6]

Dissociation: The concept dissociation was originally developed and understood as a defence against traumatic incidents by the philosopher, psychologist and therapist Pierre Janet at the beginning of the 1900s.[7] Today it is common to think of dissociation as a continuum where a daydream, for example, can be a mild and normal form, and split personalities (now known as dissociative identity disorder) can be more serious.[8] In general terms dissociation involves cutting off—or shutting out—thoughts, feelings, sense impressions, and memories.[9] It can be an adaptation to a traumatic situation that one cannot escape through fight or flight and be a part of the freeze reaction. Psychoanalysts have considered it a defence mechanism.[10] Maybe it can be understood as a contact style within gestalt therapy. In the work with Marianne, I think that dissociation also plays a role in confluence/differentiation. Perhaps the phenomena of belief and doubt can also be connected to dissociation to the degree that it involves shutting out uncomfortable memories and the like.

Internalised oppression: "I'm a whore" is an explicit or implicit message that Marianne has swallowed, a form of introjection. It seems connected to specific conditions in Marianne's life, but there is also a larger societal context. There are a number of processes in our societies that contribute to the oppression of women and what is considered woman-like. Much of this is unconscious, and it is often even internalised in women themselves.[11] Feminists have therefore highlighted the importance of women working with internalised oppression and the decolonisation of their minds.[12] For me—as for the first gestalt therapists and many other gestalt therapists today as well—personal and political liberation go hand in hand and therapy should contribute to both. When the sentence "I'm a whore" emerges with Marianne, I recognise the phenomenon and at the same time say and show that I don't see her that way. It is a form of aware confluence and differentiation. Eventually she also internalises another, more empathetic relationship to herself and is able to say to herself that she is okay.

Therapy as dance, journey and shared story: An important metaphor that the two authorities within the field Lakoff and Johnson identify in our culture is conversation as war.[13] This metaphor is expressed in language through formulations such as "fire away", to "defend one's position" and to "win a discussion". Etymologically speaking "debate" and "discussion" mean to strike down and shake apart. This has consequences: we see the conversation partner as an opponent and the conversation as something that must be won. What if the metaphor was conversation as dance? ask Lakoff and Johnson. In gestalt therapy dialogue is both a part of the method and the goal, and several therapists describe the therapy process precisely as a dance. That it is a journey we travel together is also something I think about in gestalt therapy and say to clients; for example, in the story "Three generations of betrayal". This implies something other than me already having arrived at a place, having reached my destination so to speak, and simply telling the client the way.

A third metaphor that is especially apparent in "Marianne's memories", is that therapy is a story that can be written by two or more authors in collaboration, namely the therapist and the client. Moreover, according to gestalt therapist Erving Polster, "Every person's life is worth a novel" and much of the therapist's work resembles that of an author.[14] It involves looking for a good story in the client's life. There are also specific examples of therapists and clients exchanging their accounts of the therapy and writing books together.[15]

Religion, rituals, and therapy: In "Marianne's memories" there is a ritual with a candle to conclude the sessions and a prayer as part of the dream work. People of all religious and non-religious faiths and worldviews come to gestalt therapy. When a client has a specific belief, I respect this as the client's subjective truth. Moreover, therapy is a collaborative project, and it can be useful to build upon the client's beliefs and practices. Sometimes the practices can be seen as experiments in gestalt therapy. Some also claim that prayer and religious rituals can be healing in themselves.[16] Etymologically words such as "holy", "whole" and "health" are related, and sometimes I have no doubt: there is something holy between us in the therapy room.

To dream on: In gestalt therapy the client and therapist explore a dream together here and now.[17] The dream can be told in present tense. As in "Marianne's memories", the therapist can also support the client to stay in the dream and continue it here and now, to dream on, so to speak. This can help make an unfinished situation more finished.

Therapy, touch, and abuse: Therapy has a problematic history regarding sexual abuse. In the beginning, Freud recognised the abuse his patients told him about during free association, but eventually he considered them as fantasies.[18] According to feminist professor of psychology and humanities Carol Gilligan and others, Freud, as a Jew in a patriarchal society, was increasingly at risk and eventually chose to betray women and give up psychoanalysis' radical potential in order to become more accepted.[19] Neither did the early gestalt therapists recognise sexual abuse. Fritz Perls claimed childhood traumas were inventions of clients who didn't want to grow up and mature.[20] Furthermore, far too often the therapy room itself has become a site of abuse over the years. A therapy form that emphasises equality and the I-Thou relationship such as gestalt therapy must also recognise the differential power and potential for abuse that is part of the therapy situation.[21]

On the other hand, it is possible that the increased focus on abuse today does something with our awareness and interpretation of different phenomena—that also has some negative consequences. For example, almost all touch in therapy rooms in the USA has become taboo, and associated with possible abuse. This is unfortunate when we know that touch is an important part of our communication that can have a range of positive effects on relationships and health.[22] This focus can potentially also contribute to false memories.

Einar Kringlen, professor in psychiatry, is one of those who urge caution so that one does not contribute to or recognise false memories of abuse. The quotes about false memories and recollection in the story are from a paper of his.[23] In several studies it has been demonstrated how easily false memories can occur.[24] Memory is creative and dynamic. What we remember is dependent on time, place, mood, etc. When I wrote this story several years after the course of therapy, it was spring once again. Marianne shared her memories with me, we created something together, and here and now I remember the first year of therapy with her the way I have written it. "Marianne's memories" are my memories.

The lifeline: Narrative exposure therapy is a standardised short-term treatment.[25] The therapist and the client create a lifeline from birth to present using objects, such as a rope, and mark positive experiences with flowers and negative experiences with stones. When the client recounts a traumatic experience, the goal is to recall the sequence of events in as great detail as possible and alternately focus on thoughts, feelings and bodily sensations from the incident. This is to achieve both exposure and habituation—that one gradually responds less to what is now irrelevant stimuli—and to integrate bodily and less conscious memories into the conscious autobiographical memory. Generally in trauma treatment, the traumatic incident is recounted in present tense—something that is also in line with gestalt therapy's here and now focus—but in the lifeline approach it is to be told in past tense precisely to highlight that it is a memory and not something that is happening here and now. This as well as other approaches can work as part of gestalt therapy, but when we borrow from other methods, it is important that we are faithful to central ideas in gestalt therapy, such as awareness of the relationship between the therapist and the client, what is happening here and now, and the paradoxical theory of change.[26]

Shame: Shame is something that runs through several of the stories—both in the clients and in myself as therapist. Charles Darwin already understood this as a universal emotion, expressed through, for example, blushing.[27] According to the psychologist Sylvan Tomkins and affect theory, shame is one of our intrinsic, physiological affects and something that serves as a brake on arousal, interest, and exploration.[28] Without shame we might transgress important boundaries and expose ourselves to danger, including rejection from our flock. A few decades ago—in books like the bestseller *Healing the Shame that Binds You*—the focus became more on shame as something toxic and oppressive for individuals.[29] Shame can be experienced as *being* bad—in contrast to guilt, which typically means that one experiences having *done* something wrong.

Over time a comprehensive gestalt literature on the topic has emerged. To the degree that shame involves the experience of boundaries, norms, and being wrong, it can be useful to work with introjection.[30] Wheeler understands shame as an experience of a rupture in our attachment to others and social support.[31] This experience itself will often be laden with shame and be masked. A therapist must be especially aware of this. I am committed to acknowledging clients who become aware that they are feeling shame. It is normal to feel shame—yes, even well-trained therapists do—so let's not be ashamed of it.[32] According to Wheeler, healing can often happen through the counter-pole of shame, which is social support and connection.

Feedback from clients: The importance of feedback is linked to gestalt therapy's emphasis on clients' subjective truth and dialogue. What is good therapy will vary from client to client. In the field of therapy more generally there has also been greater acknowledgement of the necessity of feedback.[33] That the client gives feedback and the therapist takes this into consideration is considered important to ensure a good therapeutic relationship and alliance by researchers who study the common factors in effective therapy.[34]

Supervision for therapists: All members of the Norwegian Gestalt Therapist Association (Norsk Gestaltterapeut Forening) are obliged to regularly attend supervision. This is to support us in our work and ensure the quality of the therapy we offer. In peer supervision, gestalt therapists meet and speak about client situations and counsel each other. Some of the supervision must also be with gestalt supervisors who have specialised training in gestalt supervision in addition to therapy. More information about the Norwegian Gestalt Therapist Association is available on the association's website www.ngfo.no.

Vicarious traumatisation: Therapists who have numerous heavily traumatised clients report that they themselves can experience intrusive and horrible mental images, physical reactions, and other conditions similar to what the client describes.[35] Mostly, these are short-lived but intense conditions. Therapists who experience such vicarious traumatisation can do several things:[36] First, it is important that they recognise their own reactions. Then it becomes possible to explore them with less shame, both alone and together with others. A professional network with a group of colleagues and supervision can be good support. Spending less of the workday and one's life on heavy trauma cases may also be necessary.

CHAPTER FIVE

Inside the walls

There is a visitor's room with a window, a couple of chairs, a sofa that can be turned into a bed, a closet with linen, and a note encouraging you to change the linen after use. I'm sitting on one of the chairs. Jonny is sitting on the sofa. He is one of the men who have accepted my offer for free therapy in the semi-open prison.
"I'm sceptical. I'd like to know more about this before we get started," he says. And we've started. Careful consideration and perhaps even resistance are also ways to be in contact.
"Do you have any particular questions?" I ask.
"I'm actually doing well, I'm dealing with things, I don't need support from anyone. Besides, society has already punished me, so I don't need to punish myself as well, I've learnt a lot from being locked in, I meditate, keep all negativity out. You're probably wondering what it was, drugs, but I've been punished for more than I actually did. I smuggled some stuff, but didn't know that it was strong substances, thought it was just some marijuana. Now I have one year left."
Jonny talks continuously for a long while. Sometimes the content is quite informative. But he jumps quickly from topic to topic. Sometimes it seems like there is a question in there, but no, there is no opening for a response. It becomes difficult to breathe. He keeps *all negativity out*.

I already find it tiring to be with him. Scepticism, the steady stream of monotonous words, it becomes a wall. He keeps me out. Perhaps he keeps a part of himself back as well. There are many words, but I hear very little about bodily sensations and feelings.

"Through regulating the breath and other self-control techniques I've learnt to travel mentally. I don't know if therapy will be consistent with my meditation practice."

I take a deep breath and jump in: "Gestalt therapy is all about awareness of what is happening here and now, and there are similarities with meditative practices such as Zen. Both are concerned with the body and attention to bodily sensations as well as thoughts and other phenomena. Together with you while you are talking and asking, for instance, I'm aware that I need to breathe and I take a deep breath."

Jonny keeps talking. About something else again. And hardly breathing it seems. He bends away when I bring in how I'm affected and my bodily sensations. Is this the polarisation between us? I am body and feelings, he is words and thoughts? I recognise his attitude from certain spiritual traditions, *mind over matter*, and that I then too can respond by emphasising *matter*. I listen only occasionally now. It's the only way I'm able to be with him. I'm present through looking. He is a rather muscular man in his forties or fifties. Shaved head. Some tattoos on his arms. T-shirt and sweatpants. Attractive in his own way. He sits quite still. Chest out, stomach in. Yes, he holds something back while the words flow out.

"But my wife does complain sometimes, says that nothing really touches me anymore."

So there's a wife. And this wall is being built in several relationships and situations. And he knows it.

When only ten minutes remain, I again speak up: "We have a few minutes till this session is finished. I'd like you to imagine that it is already over and you are on your way out. How has it been?"

"Well, it makes sense talking with you, and you get information about me."

Talking with you? Talking to, rather. It has been a monologue from one end to the other. How has he experienced me in all of this?

"And how is it to talk with me?" I ask.

"Me, I can talk and talk." And he continues to talk. "But I don't really know too much about you."

I cling to that. "Is there something you want to ask me?"

"It would be nice if you could present yourself, I want to have a two-way communication, not just sit here alone as something for you to analyse—I'm not interested in that." And he continues.

Is there anything I can do differently? Maybe me sitting here silently not interrupting him is my contribution to the wall?

"I hear," I interrupt him, "that you say you want a two-way communication. And then I hear that you continue to talk, a monologue, and I contribute by not interrupting. Until now."

"Yeah. That's true."

"In gestalt therapy we are also interested in how we relate to each other here and now. We can explore this more another time perhaps," I say.

"Yeah. I guess I can test it a few more sessions and then decide," he concludes.

The wall stands. And before I may potentially be allowed entry, I will be carefully evaluated. But how can that happen when I barely get a word or anything else in? I don't know if I'll manage to pass his test. Actually, I don't know if I really want to either.

Over the next few sessions Jonny continues talking and talking. He jumps from one topic to another. There are still some questions and apparent tests, but few openings for me to respond. I listen less and less. Perhaps he will soon decide to quit. I start hoping that he will. There is no change. I'm not getting through to him. The wall provokes me. It's as if *unsuccessful therapist* has been written somewhere on it. But if so, isn't it my writing? I'm staying in any case, mostly because I feel I have to, I think.

One day I decide to begin the session with an awareness exercise, something that can resemble meditation. I might be able to lure him along. My plan is to focus his attention on bodily sensations and feelings, something else than all the words and thinking. I'm trying to sneak inside the walls.

"Since you are interested in meditation, Jonny, I want to suggest that we do a guided awareness exercise, a slightly different kind of meditation than what you are accustomed to perhaps. The goal is simply to experience the situation bodily and emotionally here and now."

He closes his eyes and falls silent. Finally.

"Just be aware of how it is here and now. Feel how your breath is, how you sit, what you sense bodily. You don't have to change anything. Just be aware."

"I start regulating the breath," he says.

"Okay. So you start to regulate your breath. Just be aware. We can talk about what happens later."

"If we continue now, I will disappear mentally," he says.

It is not working, I think to myself, no attention to bodily sensations and feelings now either. Jonny continues in his own way.

"Let's talk a bit about what it was like," I suggest. "When I asked you to be bodily and emotionally aware of here and now, you started to regulate the breath and disappear mentally."

"Yes, that's how you meditate. You know that."

So he has heard something after all. He has picked up some information about me.

"You remember that I also meditate. That makes me happy, Jonny. But I meditate in a slightly different way, by being present also through bodily sensations and sense impressions."

"The physical is not so interesting. It is the mental and spiritual that is most important."

I don't want to give in now. "And to me it is the body that enables me to be fully present and experience you and the situation here and now."

We continue with the same polarisation. I am body and feelings, he is words and thoughts.

Suddenly it's quiet for a few seconds. My first impulse is that I must take the opportunity to say something about the polarisation between us, get some wise words in there, but then I wait a little. There is already something happening in the silence here. Jonny sinks slightly down.

"I haven't told you about the isolation. I started thinking about that now, as you said *fully present* perhaps."

"Will you tell me a bit more?"

"It's been a few years now. It lasted four months. I sat in solitary confinement. I had a few square metres. The windows had blinds, only slightly open, enough to know whether it was dark or light outside, no more. I was taken for a walk in a courtyard one hour per day."

Others locked him away, he made his own walls. Of course there is a reason why he has his wall, that he keeps other people and sense impressions out and bodily sensations and feelings back. And then it strikes me with full clarity and sadness: I have been yet another person who has tried to change him. I have tried to break through his wall, sneak in without his permission, attempt to get him to talk less and sense and feel more. I want to apologise, but that is perhaps more my need than his. I continue to listen instead.

"When we walked through the corridor on the way out to the yard, I could hear crying and screaming from adult men in the neighbouring cells. Grown men sobbing like children, Vikram."

He says my name, and I'm here together with Jonny. I swallow.

"Sometimes the guards tried to initiate a conversation with me walking through the corridor and in the yard—following up formal requirements to mitigate negative effects of isolation. Me, I spoke, but not about anything that mattered. They were my jailers after all. I've not talked to anyone about this, not really. I can't worry my wife and others on the outside."

A wall not merely to protect himself but also those around him.

"Grown men sobbing like children, Vikram," he repeats.

There are some norms about the strong and self-controlled man, I think to myself. *Big boys don't cry.* Perhaps even more so here in prison.

"But I meditated and could disappear up to several hours," he continues.

"What a wonderful adaptation to that situation, being able to disappear mentally like that," I say. I think it's the first time I really support his wall.

"Yeah. I survived."

"Yeah, you survived."

It looks like he swallows. He blinks his eyes. Now bodily sensations and feelings are also surfacing, now that I've stopped trying to force it.

"When you talk about the isolation, I feel something in my chest," I say. "Something is happening, compassion manifesting itself physically. And I let it happen. Here and now we can do more than survive. I see that you swallow, Jonny, and I think that you too are touched."

"Mm."

Even as men we can be touched, I think to myself. It's as if I can see his muscles soften. I hear him exhale. It's quiet for a while.

"It's as if I become aware of something else, something warmer in me," he says.

"Yes. So there are several sides of you."

He looks out through the window. Maybe there is a tear. I also direct my gaze out through the window. Sometimes we best support what is happening by being quiet, I think to myself. Sometimes bringing more attention through words to what is happening triggers something else, shame for a man who is crying for example. I let the silence take over for the words again. The trees are standing in the warm autumn sun. We sit like that for a while.

"We are approaching the end of this session, Jonny. And I wonder how it has been. You have talked about the isolation and shown a different side of you today."

"It's good to have told you about it."

"Do you have any ideas about how it could happen here and now between us?" I ask.

"I don't know. It probably helps that you're a therapist," he replies. "Why now and not earlier? I think I trust you more now. Just the fact that you keep showing up here, Vikram, session after session. That you don't give up on me."

"I won't give up on you, Jonny." My eyes are suddenly moist.

"And then it was really nice what you said, that it has probably been a helpful adaptation to the situation, the way I've done it."

Change can happen when one becomes what one is, is allowed to be what one is and not forced to be something else. The paradoxical theory of change. So simple, but so unusual and so easy to forget even for a gestalt therapist, I think to myself.

"The physical is good also. Of course it is," he continues. "I like to sense the sun against my skin. To hug my wife."

We get up and walk towards the door. "I hope that you will never have to experience isolation in that way, Vikram." He takes my hand—a big hand—and goes out. Out into the sun and the trees.

The last sentence remains with me. I hope that no one should have to experience isolation in that way. I'm here as a gestalt therapist, but now I also get engaged as a socio-legal scholar and human rights lawyer. Imprisonment does not fulfil its purpose, which is something all socio-legal scholars and criminologists know. It is an intentional affliction of pain, which leads to very little good. And solitary confinement should be used only in exceptional cases and for short periods of time, but Norwegian practice has been criticised repeatedly.

"I've thought a lot about what happened last time; you said that I have several sides. Can you say something more about that?" Jonny asks next time we meet.

"Well, in gestalt therapy we talk about polarities, different sides or aspects that are connected rather than mutually exclusive," I explain. "The different aspects can appear in different people, one aspect in you and another in me. They can also appear in one and the same person, both aspects appearing in you, for example. But because of important past experiences, we are sometimes less aware of certain aspects."

He nods. "I think I've been sensing the warm side of me a little more since our last session."

"If you want, we can explore that more here and now. One possibility is that you act out the warm side in one chair and the opposite of it in another."

"Okay."

I put forward two chairs. Jonny remains seated on the sofa—thinking, I think.

"Are you sitting and planning what will happen between the two sides? Are you acting it out in your head?" I check.

"Yeah, I think so."

"Well, the meaning of chair work and any dialogue is that you don't really know what will happen in advance. It's open. It's sufficient that you move physically to the other chair and say what comes to mind there."

"I don't think it's necessary to move physically."

We're about to polarise again. I am body and feelings, he is words and thoughts. But I'm aware of it. And I think it may be more beneficial that he becomes more aware of both sides in himself now.

"I think you're already acting out one side now, something other than the warm one. Maybe you can say what you said to me to the empty chair? Imagine the warm side of you there. Say for example that it's not necessary to move physically. It may seem strange at first, but look at it as an experiment."

"I don't have to move physically," he says.

And then he sits in the other chair. "Yes, here I'm the warmer one." He looks over at me and smiles. "It was the cold one that sat over there. Someone slightly strict and judgemental. I can feel it, as I'm sitting here. And it helps that you're here."

"I'm here," I say. It's an underdog, I think, one that needs my support and recognition to be present in this way. We all have a judge and a convicted confined in us. That Jonny has also been convicted and imprisoned in a very physical sense adds another dimension to this. Maybe the two sides can enter some sort of dialogue eventually.

"Is there anything you want to say to the cold one?" I ask.

"Listen to me before you judge me."

I nod. He has a childlike smile and a little colour in his cheeks now. Playful, I think, and serious.

I gesture for him to move to the sofa again, and he does. "Okay. I'll listen."

Then he changes back to the chair. "It's incredible. I've never experienced anything like this. My body temperature even rises as soon as I sit here. I sense something here." He places a hand on the middle of his chest.

"More feelings? A vulnerability?"

"Yes."

"I'm also touched, sense tears welling up, that I'd like to give you a hug. Can you say something about what happens with you to the other side?" I say.

"You are cold both physically and mentally."

"Yes. That's right," he replies from the sofa. "You can be taken for weak. I hold you back so you won't be exploited and harmed and wounded by others."

"Everyone doesn't want to exploit and hurt me," he says from his chair.

"Enough, enough feelings, shut up!" he commands from the sofa.

"No! I'm not finished talking and you said you would listen to me," he insists from his chair.

Great, I think to myself, a small triumph for the underdog, a new balance may be struck between these sides in him perhaps.

"It's quieter now suddenly," he says.

"Just remain in that state for a while. When you are ready, you can come out of the chair."

After a while Jonny rises. We are standing next to the chairs and sofa. "Now we can share some observations and reflections about what happened," I say.

"First and foremost, it's amazing how moving physically worked. I didn't believe you, but you're a magician, Vikram."

I laugh a little. I don't want that on me. It's important that Jonny owns the change and the secret behind the change. "I think it's rather a case of the body encompassing much magic and diversity."

"I think the warm side of me believes in the good in people, senses the body and feelings and can be vulnerable," he says. "But there's probably a burnt child there somewhere. That's why the cold one is here too."

So the wall is a firewall. Allow someone in or the vulnerable out, and he may be burnt. The cold one can be a wall.

"And I have understanding and compassion for that side as well," I say. "Both certainly have their functions. Perhaps they are also played out in different ways in different relationships and situations. At the beginning of therapy, while we still didn't know each other very well and there was less trust, you talked a lot, asked me questions, and I held myself back. Even in my breathing, I sensed it. But now I sense that even the breath is different, there is movement."

"Yeah, I was probably mostly showing the cold aspect of myself then. I had many thoughts about you during the first sessions. Many quick judgements."

"And today it was different. The warm side also took the floor and was given space. Then we become more whole as persons, both of us."

"I've got so much out of this session. I hope that you also get something out of this professionally, Vikram."

"Yes." I smile. "And most important, Jonny, is everything I get out of this as a human being. It has been beautiful to be with you in this process."

The last time we meet before Christmas, we talk about what we have done together over the past six months. We talk in particular about the two sides of him, the warm and the cold, and how the polarity affects and is affected by various relationships in prison and outside, including with his wife.

"I used to be very open and trusting when I was younger and I first met her. And then I've been burnt, especially in the shady world, I guess. And there's also been much suffering with the isolation and prison. Here I feel that it's necessary to be more protective. I just hope that the other, warmer side will still be there when I come out."

I listen to his words as well as watch how he moves his hands as he sits on the sofa.

"When you talked about the warm side now, you pointed with your hands to something that was quite close to you, within reach. I don't think that side is gone, Jonny. It sits in the body."

The session is approaching its end, and we begin to round up. We stand up and walk towards the door in the visitor's room. "So, Merry Christmas then," I say. "Merry Christmas, Vikram," he says. And then the big man opens his arms and leans towards me and hugs me and I hug him back.

* * *

Comments on "Inside the walls"

Imprisonment does not fulfil its purpose: In Norway and a number of other countries the explicit main purposes of imprisonment have been deterrence and rehabilitation. Using punishment to change behaviour contrasts with gestalt therapy's paradoxical theory of change. Moreover, socio-legal and criminological research since the mid 1900s has consistently shown that this change doesn't happen.[1] That is, there are changes, but usually the opposite of what is intended: prisoners create a defence against the afflicted pain and alienation from society. For many it involves embracing other norms and becoming part of the prison culture, so-called "prisonisation". As they get closer to release, many again adopt norms and behaviour more in line with the so-called law-abiding norms of society, but not entirely and prisonisation therefore has effects beyond the imprisonment period. Recent prison research has moved from the conclusion that "nothing works" to "something works". Individually tailored arrangements and follow up are necessary.

Isolation or solitary confinement is formally not considered punishment in Norway and should in theory only be used in exceptional cases and for short periods. But Norwegian practice has been repeatedly criticised by national and international human rights bodies.[2] There is broad consensus that isolation can be very harmful to a person's physical and mental health, and the most gruesome cases have been defined by courts as torture and other human rights violations.[3]

The wall as contact: There are several prominent contact styles in this story. The wall may involve resistance and a kind of protection from people Jonny is unsure wishes him well. It involves retroflection to the extent that he holds feelings and other aspects back in a sort of protection of himself as well as others. When I try to still focus on bodily sensations, feelings, or something similar, he bends away, a kind of deflection. The norm "big boys don't cry" contributes perhaps also to the wall and is a form of introjection. Dissociation can also play a role when he disappears mentally from the present physical surroundings. In the polarisation between us, there is also projection of our respective blind spots or shadow sides.

The wall has been a helpful adaptation for Jonny. He still has one year to serve of his sentence when the therapy begins. In such cases, one should be cautious as a therapist to not contribute to a change that will be difficult—or perhaps even harmful—for the person in the current situation. That we hopefully have managed a balancing act is hinted at towards the end of the story: Jonny is aware that he still needs to protect himself while he has also become more aware of what it is he is doing and that there is also another side to him, a side that he at least hopes to live out more when he gets out of prison.

"Mind over matter": The concept is popular within certain New Age movements as well as in popular psychology and even parts of academic psychology. Typically it implies that you can improve your physical health and other conditions through the power of positive thinking alone.[4] As I see it, "mind over matter" involves a ranking, a positive assessment of the mind as master "over" matter, which it can manipulate, an I-It relationship in Buber's terminology.[5] This is a split and a hierarchy with a long tradition in Western philosophy and psychology well exemplified with Descartes' "I think, therefore I am". The term "mindfulness" can be misleading and support such an idea. In contrast, Zen, as well as Buddhist meditation in general, and gestalt therapy are all about holistic, embodied experience.

As a gestalt therapist it is important to me to take clients' subjective reality and truth as a starting point. For Jonny "mind over matter" has been a helpful adaptation. Yet, I am concerned about the inseparable integrity of mind and body and that we don't rank and split up aspects of ourselves. Through an aware and dialogical approach, it seems that there is some integration of the polarity in Jonny as well.

"Big boys don't cry": Many adults in western culture find crying problematic, especially men. Psychotherapist and historian of ideas Claes Ekenstam shows how this is historically and culturally contingent.[6] In earlier periods, a man who wept was positively assessed. After a close friend was killed in battle, Achilles in Homer's Iliad threw himself on the ground, tore at his hair, screaming and crying—without it being considered unmanly. By the 1800s with industrialisation, urbanisation and the emerging bourgeoisie, male crying had been feminised and pathologised. While sexual self-control was demanded of women, emotional self-control was required of men. In with the stomach and out with the chest was the instruction in books on etiquette. That also does something with men's emotional life and expression. We see important changes today, but the norm is still strong, perhaps especially in certain environments such as in male prisons.

CHAPTER SIX

Put on your own mask first

"I struggle with my self-image. I was bullied a lot as a kid," he says.
It has been a long, dark winter day, and Eric is my last client before the day is over. I feel the need to yawn, but am afraid that he will take it personally and think that I find him boring or difficult.

"I'm a little tired today. That's why I just yawned. I just wanted to clarify. And I'd very much like to hear more, Eric."

"We can always change our session if you're tired," he suggests.

"I appreciate your consideration, but it's fine for me to be a bit tired. You can also be tired here. We are here as whole human beings."

We smile to one another.

"How do you feel right here and now with me?" I ask.

"I already feel relaxed."

"Can you say more about that? How do you feel relaxed in your body, for example?"

"My breathing is calm, my shoulders loose," he says.

I smile and nod.

"I'd also like to hear more about the bullying and your self-image that you mentioned. If you want to?"

"It began in primary school and continued all the way through high school."

So many years with bullying. Horrible. But at the same time Eric continues to speak in such general terms that I'm not completely drawn in. Not one word about him being gay, for example, but he is, isn't he? When he first reached out by email, he said that he'd read an interview with me on gaysir.no. This website doesn't have many straight readers. And homo tops the list of insults in school along with Sami, Jew and whore. He could be Sami or Jewish, I guess.

"I don't know how much I should say. I think that it's affected me quite a lot," he says.

"You don't need to say more than you want. We don't know each other so well yet. And we have time to explore this more together. How does it feel now to have told me a little about the bullying? How do you experience our relationship so far?" I ask.

"Good. You're very skilled at creating a good relationship."

"That's nice to hear. Still, I think that we both create this relationship together," I say. "By the way, self-image can also be understood relationally and socially. It's about a relationship you have to yourself, how you see yourself. But this often also involves what you think others think about you. Are you wondering what I have thought so far?"

"Did you notice something with my body a moment ago that I wasn't aware of?" he asks. "Did you think that I actually wasn't relaxed?"

"No, I also thought you looked relaxed," I reply. "I was simply curious about how *relaxed* is experienced bodily for you. In gestalt therapy we are interested in holistic awareness. I'm glad that you ask, by the way. I hope that you can feel okay to check your interpretations with me, that this becomes a safe place."

"Yeah. Ugh! I interpret quite a lot when I'm with people without checking if the interpretations are correct," he says.

"I think we all do that. Myself included," I say.

Of course we all have certain things we do better and certain things we do worse. Is it possible for him to see both in himself?

"I'm a little curious about what you think you are good at, Eric. Can you list two or three things you believe that you can do well?"

"Well, I'm a control freak," he replies.

Pretty negatively loaded. Is that the closest he can get to saying something positive about himself?

"And I have pretty good—okay, here comes some bullshit words—intuition and gut feeling."

I notice that I tense my muscles a little, as if somebody is about to punch me. Eric has become his own bully. Is he aware of this relationship?

"Some bullshit words," I repeat. "For you, intuition and gut feeling are true and important, right?"

"Yes."

"And still you present them that way, introduce them with *here comes some bullshit words*."

"Yeah, that was silly of me." He hits himself on the head, and then he hits himself on the head even more when I point out that he's hitting himself on the head. It's hard to witness. I need to be cautious. Maybe the best I can do now is to help normalise the shame, this terrible feeling of being wrong. At the same time I can be explicit about being gay, open up to that topic.

"Eric, I also do that sometimes. Personally I have become more aware that I feel shame in different situations. For example, I can feel it when I walk hand in hand with my partner in public. And since open and proud gays aren't supposed to feel shame, I can easily feel ashamed of the shame as well."

The session continues for a while. I don't get much more information about the bullying. Afterwards I re-read the interview with me on gaysir.no to see what Eric has read, and perhaps get some clues about him. In the interview I particularly spoke about mental health among gay people and how this is linked with the larger societal context. I talked about shame, my own included. Had I been born three years earlier, I would have had a diagnosis; eight years earlier and I would have been a criminal.

Today's Norway is radically different. Still, negative, more or less conscious attitudes towards gay people remain widespread, even internalised in ourselves against ourselves. For some clients who belong to a sexual or gender identity minority, it matters that I too belong to such a group. I'm convinced of that. It may not be that these issues are always explored directly and explicitly, but our minority identities and attitudes connected to them are always there as part of the background—so it is with Eric as well, I think.

He arrives precisely on time and takes his shoes off outside the door. "That way I don't mess up your foyer with this winter weather." Always considerate.

"Thanks. I appreciate that," I say.

We make small talk while he takes off his coat. Then we enter the therapy room and sit down.

"How are you doing?" he asks.

The eternal question of how much I should self-disclose. I've said that we can be whole human beings together, and I want to show that everything is not always great with me either. I also want to show that I appreciate his question and his consideration.

"It's a bit difficult between me and my partner right now, so I'm feeling a little low. But right now when you ask me, Eric, and I experience that you are interested in me, I also feel happy."

"Sorry to hear about you and your partner. I hope it works out." The tone, body language, everything about him makes me believe that he really means that. Eric is considerate.

"Thanks. I hope so too. And how are you doing?"

"Well, I've actually had a difficult time as well," he says. "It's not really a boyfriend, but a guy I dated for a while and then he didn't want to anymore."

So he is gay, or dates men at least. Maybe it helped that I shared a little from my life. In any case, Eric is telling me more now.

"He was in the closet. I'm often with men who are in the closet, by the way. I don't make a big deal about being gay myself. Almost nobody at work knows about it. It's not like I'm hiding it, but I just don't see the point in telling everyone either."

Coming out of the closet is a continual process in a society where most people have as a starting point that we are all straight, I think. We constantly choose to either come out or not, and this doesn't only depend on ourselves, but on the particular situation and if there is support available. I can understand that not all of Eric's colleagues know. For a long time, there were many people around me who also didn't know that I was gay. I said to myself that sexual orientation wasn't such a defining aspect, but I never fully convinced myself that it wasn't also due to shame. I continue listening to Eric. At some point he mentions something about self-loathing.

"I'm curious about that word, *self-loathing*. When do you feel that? In which relationships and settings?" I ask.

"With dating and at work, for instance," he replies.

"If you want, we can explore this further here and now. We can use some chairs and imagine that you are on a date or at work," I suggest.

"Okay."

I want to ensure that Eric really wants to do this if we are to do it; that he doesn't just do it to please me.

"What are you sensing right now in your body, Eric, when I suggest this?"

"I feel tingling. I want to try."

"Okay. Then you can place a couple of those empty chairs however you wish in the room, and sit in one of them."

Eric stands up, organises two chairs in the room, and sits down in one of them.

"Are you on a date or at work now?" I ask.

"A date," he replies. "But it's difficult to imagine somebody there in the other chair."

My chest and stomach tighten. Eric is sitting there alone on the date.

"I'm not getting anywhere. Can we try work instead?" he asks.

"Yeah."

It goes quiet.

"This is also difficult," he says.

"That's perfectly okay. Maybe we don't know who is sitting in the other chair."

After a while he offers a description: "faceless."

The bully or bullies, I say to myself. Perhaps also the faceless mob that simply stand idly by and is passively a part of it. Something unfinished in Eric's life is still pressing and emerges in new situations and relationships. Maybe this can be the necessary confrontation, a resolution.

"Are you aware of something more now that you sit in front of this faceless person?" I ask. "Maybe some bodily sensations, feelings, thoughts in the form of voices or images? Impulses to do something?"

"My heart is racing. I want to run away. But I also want to stay here. I want to be a human being."

"Maybe you can say that to the faceless person," I suggest.

"I want to be a human being." It goes quiet again. Then he looks at me. "It's quiet now."

"Do you want to ask who is in the other chair?" I ask.

"No."

"Okay," I say. "It's good that you know what you want and do it."

I'm curious, but that is my own need. Maybe it's also too emotional and unsafe to go further at this point in time. Regardless, it is significant in itself that Eric now finds himself in a relationship where his "No" is respected.

"Do you want to get up from the chair so we can talk about what happened and what we think about it?" I ask.

Eric slowly gets up. We stand beside each other and look at the chairs.

"I've been affected by the bullying," he says.

"Yes. And I also observed that now you remained in front of the faceless person without running away. And I heard you say that you want to be a human being."

"Yes."

"It's a bit abstract, but it's as though I glow when I leave this place. That's a silly word, *glow*. But it's something that you have done, Vikram, that has changed me. You're so clever."

"I feel a little split when you say that, Eric. I'm happy and at the same time I think that this is something that we do together, that I'm not changing you."

Maybe he can own a bit of the projection. Maybe I can throw it back at him. "That's fantastic, Eric, what you've done that makes you glow and change!"

He moves in his chair. Bends away. "By the way, do you ski? I thought I saw some skis in the foyer a moment ago."

"I notice that you are moving in your chair and I hear that you are starting to talk about something else now," I say. "When you are in the spotlight, receive some recognition, it seems that you dodge away. You depend on people around you for affirmations. But at the same time you also have a responsibility of choosing to accept or not accept these, and stay or rather set the spotlight on others than yourself."

"That makes sense. I focus a lot on others."

I get an idea for an experiment. Projection—to throw something out to another—and to receive and take ownership of something is a metaphor we can also examine concretely and physically.

"Do you want to play a bit? We've done a lot of talking." I get a little pillow. He smiles. "I give you a compliment when I throw the pillow to you, and you can answer yes or no after considering the pillow and the compliment. If it's a yes, you keep the pillow for a moment before you throw it back with a compliment about me. If it's a no, then throw it right back with your no."

"Okay."

"You dress well," I say and throw the pillow.

"No," Eric says and throws the pillow back.
"You have nice eyes."
"No."
And so we continue with compliments and throwing for a while.
"You are considerate."
"Yes," he finally says and keeps the pillow.

We smile to one another. So there is something positive that he can identify with, *considerate*. That makes sense.

"I wonder if we should stop the throwing game now," I suggest. "Would you like to formulate it as a full sentence *Yes, I am considerate*?"

"Yes, I am considerate."

"How did that feel?"

"It feels right. And I also feel warmer and more playful."

This experiment, mobilising the entire body and not just the thoughts, opened up the way for something new. A friendlier voice, different from the self-critical one, is emerging.

We remain seated in silence. Eric looks at me, dark eyes in an otherwise light and young man. He breathes calmly.

"I become aware of your calm breathing and your dark eyes, Eric." I should stay as close to sense impressions as possible, I think now. This is something other than compliments and judgements like saying that he dresses well or has nice eyes. I draw him in a different way. A different image emerges.

"I also see your blonde hair, a few freckles on your nose, a light collar and a newly ironed shirt," I continue.

He smiles.

"How does it feel to be seen this way?" I ask.

"Good," he replies.

We sit in silence once more.

"And how is this quietness?"

"I like it. I do it from time to time," he says.

"I'm happy when you tell me what you like and what you do, Eric. It allows me to see you even more clearly."

"I probably do focus on others a lot. I've thought a little about this since the last session," he says. "Maybe I should be more considerate of myself as well."

"Can you try to say *I want to be considerate of myself* and see how this feels? If it rings true?"

"I want to be considerate of myself." He smiles.

"You're smiling. How did it feel?" I ask.

"It feels much more powerful to say it like that. But not just good. I don't like the narcissistic culture we live in. It's always about me, me, me."

"Yeah, I completely agree."

"The need to be famous just for the sake of being famous," he says.

"Everyone is so special and unique, overinflated egos from birth to death," I say.

In the worst case, I think therapy can also create more overinflated egos, especially therapy that focuses on enhancing self-esteem. And there are experts who actually link bullying to narcissism, that bullying can be a way for vulnerable, inflated egos to protect themselves. Eric has been bullied—and one part of him now bullies another part.

"The facades on Facebook," he continues.

"Monologues about me," I say.

We sit like this for a while, a form of confluence, us two against the narcissistic society. Yet, can we also eventually integrate some of this pole? I make an attempt. "I want to be considerate of others and I also want to be considerate of myself. That's true for me. Do you want to try to say something like that and see how it feels for you, Eric?"

"I want to be considerate of others and I also want to be considerate of myself," he says.

"Maybe this is a polarity, two poles that are complementary and connected rather than in an opposing, mutually exclusive relationship. By becoming more aware of the less known side—being considerate towards yourself—maybe you can experience yourself in a different way. Maybe it can even develop further the other side, being considerate to others."

While talking I again become aware of the sensitivity for anything that can be interpreted as criticism. Is what I'm saying making Eric think that he's doing even more things wrong, that he should do something or be different than he is? I'm not a good enough therapist. Then I become aware of that as well, shame, that it is also something occurring between us.

"But this isn't about you needing to be reprogrammed, Eric. Saying this sentence is only an experiment to see how it feels," I say. "In a way, on one level, I think that you are perfectly fine as you are and don't need to change anything about yourself. If we can just get to know you better, as you already are."

Eric smiles.

"What happens when I say this?" I ask.

"I think that it's somewhat a lie. A part of me feels that I'm insufficient, that what you're saying you say as a professional. But it's also nice to hear."

I get an idea. There is something we can do, something that builds upon his considerateness rather than him inflating himself or being inflated by me.

"Part of you says that you're insufficient, and a part feels that it was nice to hear. I just got an idea about something we could try, something that builds upon your considerateness. Metta, or loving-kindness, is a meditation where you first wish yourself well, and then another person or being that you care for, then a familiar stranger, and then you can expand it to include more and more. We can try it together if you want? When we do this as an experiment in gestalt therapy, the only goal is to have a new experience here and now, to explore and become aware of what we feel and do. Just see what happens. There is nothing that is right and wrong."

"I'd like to try." Eric smiles.

"Then you can begin by sitting in a way that allows you to be both comfortable and alert. You can close your eyes or rest your gaze a little in front of you on the floor if you wish."

Eric closes his dark eyes. I also close mine.

"First you can place a hand on your chest. Sense the touch. On your chest you sense the light pressure from your hand. On your palm you sense your chest, maybe also your heart beating. Take a moment to sense this. What does this do with you already, this light touch from yourself?" I say. "Now you can imagine that you wish yourself well. If it helps, you can imagine that you see yourself sitting on a chair in front of you, and repeat these sentences in your mind: May you be safe. May you have good health. May you be happy. May you be free. Become a little aware of how it is to wish yourself well in this way, how you experience it bodily, if there is a particular state of mind, any particular thoughts. You can again rest your hand on your lap."

I let it be quiet a moment.

"Now you can choose another being, a person or animal, that you care about. It can also be somebody you don't know personally. There are perhaps many, but choose only one now. Imagine that this other being is sitting here in a chair in front of you."

Occasionally, I open my eyes and am aware of Eric. But I also participate in the meditation. Now I am imagining my partner.

"You can imagine that you send good wishes out from your heart when exhaling, or that you are whispering them to the other. May you be safe. May you have good health. May you be happy. May you be free. Again become a little aware of how it is to wish another well in this way, how you experience it bodily, if there is a particular state of mind, any particular thoughts." I say and again let it be quiet for a moment.

"Now you can imagine somebody that you have a more neutral relationship to, somebody that you neither like nor dislike particularly. Maybe somebody who lives in the same building or somebody who works in the shop where you usually do your grocery shopping, a familiar stranger. Again imagine this person in front of you here and send out good wishes."

I open my eyes and look at Eric. He's breathing calmly. When I close them again, I still see Eric. I wish him well. "May you be safe. May you have good health. May you be happy. May you be free. Again become aware of how it is to wish this other well." This also does something with our relationship, I think, me wishing him well affects me and thereby how I am with him.

The next step in metta is to include a person one has a difficult relationship with, but I think it's too early for this. Yes, we'll stop here for now.

"Now you may again become aware of the chair you're sitting on, the floor under your feet, your breathing, and eventually open your eyes. You don't need to share everything you experienced, but maybe you want to say something about how the experience was, something you became particularly aware of."

Eric opens his eyes. They're dark, but have a sort of light inside them now.

"The best part was wishing a stranger well," he says. "I felt it like an expansion in my chest."

I smile. I recognise that sensation.

"And how was it for you that the meditation began by wishing yourself well? How did that feel?"

"It was okay," he replies. "I know that it's important to consider oneself. Put on your own oxygen mask before assisting others."

After the session I think about this metaphor. It's a good image, one that suits Eric well. It shows that taking care of oneself is necessary in order to take care of others. And being considerate is something that is important to him. At the same time, I think that it is also vice versa, that taking care of others is necessary for taking care of oneself. Research shows that we become happier when we are considerate of others. These are complementary poles, a polarity.

Put on your own mask first. I get several associations to theatre and chair work and smile to myself. *Faceless* was something that came up in our chair work together. And what about being in the closet? Being able to hide partially or completely using a disguise can also be useful in some situations. Yet at the same time, I find that Eric and his face are becoming clearer to me. *I want to be a human being.* We become whole human beings.

"Vikram, I was wondering if we could do that meditation again?" he asks during the next session.

But then it becomes more of an exercise, is my first thought, and that's not really in line with gestalt therapy, is it?

"It gave me a lot, and I want to try to do it regularly," he continues. "If you guide me one more time, I can try to remember the various steps to use later."

On the other hand, this is something he wants, I think to myself, and it's a good thing to put Eric and his needs in focus. Besides, personally I do metta regularly.

"We can record it so that you don't need to sit and remember the instructions for later," I suggest.

"Oh, that would be great!"

I activate the voice recorder on my iPhone and begin the meditation. This time I also include the final step.

"Now you can imagine somebody who you have a more difficult relationship to. If this is too much for you at this point, leave it for now. Check what is okay for you here and now. But if it is okay, you can perhaps also recognise that this person too wants safety and good health, wants happiness and strives to be free, just like all the rest of us. Imagine the other person in a chair at a distance that feels okay for you."

Maybe it is the faceless one, I wonder. I open my eyes and see Eric. He is breathing calmly. It's okay. I go into the exercise myself as well, and all of a sudden I remember a bullying incident, an instance of homophobia. A middle-aged man started yelling at me and my partner while I slept in his arms on a bus just the other day.

"May you also be safe. May you have good health. May you be happy. May you be free. Again become aware of how it is to wish this other well, a person you have a more difficult relationship to."

I let it be quiet a moment. "Finally imagine all of the world's beings, everything that exists, in one form or another, maybe as a person or an animal or a tree, maybe the entire blue planet seen from space. Can you wish everything and everybody well? How does this feel? Now just sit for a while and become aware of whatever you are experiencing. Then open your eyes when you are ready."

After a minute Eric opens his eyes. "I feel relaxed. My heart rate is slow. It felt good to wish everyone and everything well. To see that we all have those needs. And I can also get used to wishing myself well. I have to put on my own mask before assisting others. This has become clearer to me. It feels like I'm going down another direction now, Vikram. The old road was self-loathing; the new road is having good feelings towards myself as well."

More about the person or persons Eric had a difficult relationship with I will never know. A few days later he calls and thanks me for the therapy and informs me that he will continue working with these issues on his own for a while now. I never find out more about the faceless one. Then half a year later I get an email. Eric is feeling better. While at the beginning of the therapy I thought that there would be a necessary confrontation with demons from his past through the empty chair, in the email he confirms that it was especially metta that has helped him:

> It helps me in my relationships to others and my relationship to myself. I can see myself a little from the outside using metta. I can even wish my inner critic well, the internal voice that is very critical to myself. I see that it only wants safety as well. This is maybe a little clumsily communicated, but ... I also liked your way of being, Vikram. You are genuinely interested in the person sitting in front of you. P.S. I am together with a great guy now. P.P.S. I hope that it is going well with you and your partner as well!

I catch myself smiling a little when I read "a little clumsily communicated, but ..." Yet he doesn't appear to be nearly as self-critical as before. And I appreciate his generosity to me. I have enjoyed being together with Eric. I wish him well. Much of what we did together—and much of therapy in general—is about this, I think, about caring, compassion, and self-compassion. And it seems that this became Eric's resolution with the faceless one.

* * *

Comments on "Put on your own mask first"

Bullying and homophobia: Sexual minorities are especially exposed to bullying. According to one study, half of gay boys in Norway are bullied two to three times each month at school, and "homo" and similar words are common insults.[1] Furthermore, there are correlations between having been exposed to bullying and experiencing anxiety and depression. Being exposed to bullying and experiencing anxiety can additionally contribute to the person himself bullying others. This is a possible explanation for why gay boys are also overrepresented among those who bully, according to the same study. Those who bully also have the need for safety, good health, to be happy, and to be free.

In Norway, homosexuality was criminalised until 1972, and given a psychiatric diagnosis until 1977. Many people still have negative, more or less conscious attitudes that can manifest through overt and direct acts or omissions or more subtle microaggressions.[2] Unfortunately, this also includes some therapists. The less conscious attitudes can be revealed through tests at www.projectimplicit.net, the webpage of Project Implicit, one of the world's largest psychological experiments and studies. Even myself, an open gay man who comes from a relatively progressive family, received the following conclusion: "Your data suggest a strong automatic preference for Straight People compared to Gay People". This was an eye opener to just how pervasive and internalised homophobia still is and how important it is to continue addressing this, including through therapy. One of the founders of gestalt therapy, Paul Goodman, was an open bisexual and was dedicated to liberating sexual minorities as well as the heterosexual majority through queer politics.[3]

The self and self-image: In the West the self has for a long time been seen as a relatively stable and internal structure. In gestalt therapy the self is rather conceptualised as a process. Instead of nouns, it is therefore more precise to use verbs such as "selfing", something many Buddhists also do. According to *Gestalt Therapy*, selfing continuously occurs through contact here and now.[4] The authors describe three important factors in the process: "it" ("id") involves sensations and experiences of what is needed in a particular situation; "I" ("ego") involves choice and action; and "me" ("personality") points to the experience of who I become/am. A dialogical perspective would additionally emphasise the relational aspect of selfing. In line with polarity theory, one can also understand selfing as a diversity of complementary sides and forces in and between us. However, since phenomenology is a basis of gestalt therapy, therapists should start from a person's own experience and subjective truth, regardless of other theories. If a client experiences having an internal and stable self—a common Western point of view—I will therefore also respect this.

"Self-image" and "self-esteem" can be similar to the "me" factor in the gestalt theory. It refers to how I see myself. A relationship is also found here: I-me. A critical, compassionate or another type of relationship can colour this image. Because we are influenced by relationships with others, the image I have of myself will also be influenced by how others see me—or more accurately, how I believe that they see me. According to sociologist Charles Cooley, this is what's known as "the looking glass self".[5]

The narcissistic culture: The cultural historian Christopher Lasch concluded that the American post-war era's late capitalistic culture had become narcissistic.[6] He described several phenomena, including increased emphasis on individuals over families and society, weak experiences of the self, constant searching for external affirmation, need for acknowledgement and fame, fleeting and superficial relationships, lack of impulse control, and that one sees the world as merely a mirror for oneself. These are phenomena that have only become clearer in our times, also in Norway.

There is much written about narcissism in general, and definitions and evaluations of the phenomenon vary. The gestalt therapist Gary Yontef recognises that we all have different degrees of narcissistic vulnerability and believes that important components include preoccupation with one's own self-image, shame and self-criticism that often in turn is projected onto others.[7] As a gestalt therapist, it is also tempting to connect narcissism to I-It relationships and Martin Buber's dialogical philosophy.[8] Several psychologists and therapists believe that bullying can be linked to a high degree of narcissism.[9]

"Around the world" phenomenon: By becoming more aware of a less known pole—for example, for Eric to be considerate towards himself—the counter-pole can also develop—for Eric, being considerate towards others. Gestalt therapist Joseph Zinker describes this as the "around the world" phenomenon: if you go far enough North you will eventually be going South.[10] This can also be understood in light of the paradoxical change theory. Additionally, Zinker connects work with polarities to "self-concept"—a concept closely linked to, if not the same as, self-image. He claims that we get a healthier and more whole self-concept through increased awareness of all the different sides and forces within us.

Happiness research: Over time, a field known as positive psychology has emerged within academic psychology. The research focus has been well-being and happiness, whilst psychology has traditionally primarily dealt with pathology and suffering. A number of studies now show that we can become happier by being friendly and generous with other people.[11] This is why there is now solid support for Dalai Lama's challenge to selfish people to be "wisely selfish", focusing on the well-being of others.[12]

Metta: Metta or "loving-kindness" is a classical Buddhist meditation that draws on scriptures such as Karaniya Metta Sutta.[13] The meditation teacher Sharon Salzberg played a central role in introducing this to the West.[14] Over time, research conducted by professor in psychology Barbara Fredrickson and others has revealed that this type of meditation can result in positive emotions, increased well-being, and a number of health benefits.[15] As a gestalt therapist I sometimes suggest metta as an experiment. In the story with Eric, this also became more of an exercise. Metta has similarities with chair work. One imagines oneself—or a part of oneself—or another and enters a form of compassionate relationship with this other. Of course one can also do this with open eyes and facing an actual chair. Classical chair work will also often result in both increased compassion and self-compassion.[16] You may not be walking in another's shoes, but you are sitting in the other's chair.

Self-esteem and self-compassion: Therapists and psychologists have long been occupied with self-esteem. It can be understood as a positive evaluation of oneself and positive feelings such as pride associated with this evaluation. Today much research—such as that by Kristin Neff—shows the advantages of self-compassion over self-esteem.[17] Enhancing self-esteem can lead to greater self-occupation in a negative sense and is not robust in the face of adversity. In other words, it resembles narcissism.

In contrast, self-compassion contributes to increased compassion with others as well as oneself and is more stable in both prosperity and adversity. Self-compassion also has many advantages over carrot and stick methods for change and is more effective in the long term. When we do not fear mistakes and defeat quite as much, we are freer and more willing to try something. As occasional mistakes and defeats unavoidably occur, they then become opportunities for self-compassion and learning rather than punishment and worse self-esteem.

Gestalt therapy's dialogical relationship, awareness and recognition of existential conditions such as imperfection resemble the three elements that Kristin Neff identifies in self-compassion—namely, kindness, mindfulness, and recognition of our common humanity. She also builds upon Buddhist practices, including metta, and even uses gestalt-inspired chair work.[18]

CHAPTER SEVEN

Freeze

"I pack it down and hold it inside." With her hands she also shows how she packs down and holds it inside. As usual, Nina sits in front of me dressed in black. Black says something too, I think to myself.

"It has worked pretty well," she continues. "I have control. But lately I've experienced sudden and impulsive outbursts, anger and the like. They just come out of nowhere." She demonstrates by flinging her hand up, up from whatever she has packed down, perhaps.

"This makes me curious. Chair work?" I suggest. She has already been going to gestalt therapy a while—both with me and with others.

"Yes, here we can explore it. This is a safe space."

She gets two empty chairs, places them in the middle of the room, and sits down in one of them.

"There's the person I hate." She points to the chair in front of her and looks at me.

"Is there anything you want to say or do now?" I ask. "Check with yourself. How does it feel inside your body?"

She is a thin girl in her mid twenties. Now she appears even smaller. She sits bent forward as though she's protecting her stomach area, supports her head with her hands, elbows on her knees. I'm also sitting like this in a chair beside her.

"I sense that I'm not breathing deeply, that it's mostly chest and neck," I say.

"Yes. Me too," she says. "Whenever I inhale I sense what is down there, a lump in my stomach. I can't stand breathing all the way down and feeling it."

"Okay. Just follow yourself and your needs, Nina."

"I've always thought that I would attack the person."

"Can we put something on the empty chair that can better symbolise the person? This pillow for example? Then we can see what you want to do with it here and now."

"Okay."

I get the pillow and put it there. "What are you feeling now? What do you get the urge to do? And what do you do?"

She sits quietly.

"You're not saying anything. You're sitting there quietly."

"I'm a coward," she says.

"You're a coward, you say. What I see is you sitting quietly. This can also be a skilful way of responding. And you told me that you have an angry side, outbursts, that you can also burst out."

"Yes, Angry-Nina."

"Should we put her somewhere in this room?" I ask.

"Okay."

"Which colour suits her?"

"Black."

I get a black blanket. "Like this?"

"Yes." She takes the blanket, puts a third chair in the room and spreads the black blanket over the chair.

So now we have a triangle of chairs here: The One I Hate symbolised by a pillow, Angry-Nina with the black blanket, and an empty white chair where Nina was just sitting and considered herself a coward. We remain standing and observe the three chairs.

"While he came into me, she comes out of me." She nods towards the One I Hate and Angry-Nina.

Rape, I think, but try to put the assumption aside and remain open.

"Can you sit there for a moment?" I point to Angry-Nina's chair.

"No, I can't be her now. Maybe I see her a little better, but I don't understand her. She's so unpredictable."

"Okay. Should we clear away these chairs and talk a little about what has happened?"

"Okay."

We sit down by the window again in the therapist and client chairs.

"It feels calmer in my head. Usually there are only a bunch of black scribbles in there. Now we have taken out two of the scribbles, the One I Hate and Angry-Nina," she says.

On the way out she gives me a hug. Nina always gives me a hug when she comes and a hug when she goes.

"The framework has become loose," she says the next time we meet. "The head doesn't know where to sit."

The framework, I imagine it, a little fragile.

"I was at a dinner with my best friend last weekend. I said that I had pain in my neck," she continues.

Not uncommon, I think, with tensions and pains in the body when one is holding so much back over time.

"Suddenly some guy is standing behind me and pulling my shoulders backwards because he thought I was hunched too much forward, that this was the reason for the pain. Now I'm irritated."

"And what did you do when he came to pull your shoulders backwards?"

"Nothing. I let him do it."

"I suggest an experiment." I get up and place myself as far away as possible from her in the room. "I will start over here. I will move slowly towards you and I want you to sense through your body how this feels, if there's a particular point, a place, where you feel that I should stop, and see what you do about it. What do you say?"

"Okay."

"I see that something is happening with you. Can you describe what is happening?"

"I'm breathing more rapidly. I don't know where I should look. I'm laughing."

"Yes. Good that you can be aware of that." I move even closer. "Can you tell me when I have come close enough or too close?"

She doesn't reply.

"I'll move a little back again," I say and do so.

"I don't know what happened," she says.

"I think you went into freeze, a common reaction to something that is perceived as uncomfortable or dangerous."

I sit down in the chair in front of her again.

"Do you sense the chair and the floor now?" I ask.

"I sense them when you ask me to. But it feels like it's somebody else's body. I'm the head. The body simply takes me where I need to go."

"And how do you feel about body contact?"

"I've always hated physical contact. I always look forward to the point where the first phase in a relationship is over, when we don't need to be so physical anymore. My partner and I are there now," she says.

"And yet you give me a hug before and after our sessions."

"Yes."

"I wonder if this is something you feel that you should do. I don't need a hug. I'm interested in you becoming more aware of your needs together with me."

"Yeah."

We small talk a while before we conclude the session. On the way out the door Nina gives me a hug.

"It exploded again last Friday," she says. Angry-Nina has been relegated to *it* again, to the body.

"Can you try to say, *I exploded last Friday*? See how that feels?"

"I exploded. I exploded because I was afraid."

"You exploded because you were afraid," I repeat.

"Yes, that's right. That's how it is. I want to tell you about Friday." I nod, and she continues the story.

"I was together with my partner. He got drunk. I didn't want him to have more to drink. He seemed distant. He continued to drink. Then he wanted to have sex. He pulled me into the living room and threw me on the sofa. I just had to lie down flat."

I imagine the thin, black-dressed figure lying flat on the sofa or the ground and a drunk man hovering over her.

"I felt scared and helpless and then it went black. I got angry. I flailed with my arms. And he hit."

"He threw you onto the sofa. You flailed with your arms. And he hit," I repeat.

"Yes. It is wrong." This sounds like something she knows that she should say.

"He's very sorry afterwards," she continues. "He needs help. He has an alcohol problem."

"It may very well be that he is suffering and needs to find help," I say. "Regardless, I think that we should place the responsibility for what happened between you two on him."

It's painful to see that Nina is in a violent relationship. Her partner is probably struggling with something himself —it's not uncommon that those who exercise violence or otherwise breach another's boundaries have themselves experienced much suffering—but it's Nina who is going to therapy with me now. She is my focus.

"I've heard that you can both lie flat and freeze in the face of danger and become angry, fight. Maybe Angry-Nina has a function. You exploded because you were afraid, as you yourself said. How does it feel to hear this?"

"It's good that you say that. Earlier I've felt a little resistance when Angry-Nina has been given a place here in the room. But now I'm beginning to get to know her a little better, this side of myself."

Nina and I meet weekly; she is dressed in black and hugs me every time. Soon it is our final session before Christmas.

"My mom has been visiting. She's ill again," she says.

"Okay. How does that feel for you?"

"I've been diagnosed with cancer." She says this as if she is going to the shop to buy something and they're all sold out. Packed down, controlled.

"With my mom, the conversation quickly went over to focusing on her again," she continues. "At one point I got angry at her, and it felt good."

"That's good that you're aware of how you feel and what you need, Nina. That you're more in touch with your anger as well and can direct it outward when necessary."

"Yes."

"And I'm saddened to hear about your cancer diagnosis, but I'm mostly concerned with how this feels for you," I continue.

"I'm pretty distanced from it all. I don't know."

"Maybe that's what you need right now. Otherwise it might have been too much at once. You can also pack down and hold back. This can be useful too."

It goes quiet for a moment.

"I'm so tired, Vikram."

When I support her in what she does, a counter-pole to packing down emerges. I think to myself that she now does sense how she feels, tired now, and expresses it together with me.

"Is there something we can do together when you are tired, Nina? Can you rest? Would you like to lie down here a moment?"

"Mom said, *It's always so good coming to you, Nina, because you pick me up.*"
"How did that feel for you?"
"I got irritated."
"Okay."
"I tend to compensate when I'm tired by working more."
"So when you are tired, you work more," I repeat.

Nina exhales. Again a small change, one that begins with her breath.

"I hear that you are exhaling now, Nina. Can you do this more and just follow with the rest of your body. See where the movement takes you."

She puts her head down on her knees for a brief moment, but then lifts it quickly up again. "I relax when I sleep. I want to sleep all the time."

"Do you?"

"No. I don't want to be like them, like my mom and my aunt. They sleep. They are so weak and helpless. I'm afraid that if I don't compensate I'll never be able to get up again."

"I know that you can be active and strong," I say. "Maybe you have projected the counter-pole onto your mother and aunt. It may be that it fits well on them, but maybe it's interesting to explore this side in yourself as well. Maybe sometimes it can be good to rest and sleep."

"I'm going to my mom and aunt this Christmas. It would definitely be something new if I didn't take all of the responsibility, but instead lay down and slept a bit. Maybe I'll do that."

After the session I remain in my chair and think about Nina. I hope that she gets to rest during Christmas, but I also wonder what might pop up while she is at home with her mother and aunt. Yes, pop up, because there is something that is still being held down. The One I Hate, it's still not completely clear who this is and what has happened between them.

It's Christmas, and then a new year.

"I slept. I did. And it was good," she says.

Then it goes quiet.

"What is happening with you now?" I want to check if this is freeze or just silence.

"It's silent."

"Okay. That's fine with me, silence."

Outside it's snowing.

"It's not really silent," she says. "There are black scribbles in the head."

She has mentioned something about this before. Wasn't the One I Hate and Angry-Nina two such scribbles, something that she had packed down and held in for a long time?

"How do they look?" I ask.

"Like children's drawings. As a kid I received a box of coloured markers and paper from mom one year for Christmas. I drew black scribbles when I was angry or sad. I coloured them when I was happy. Over time it became only more and more black scribbles. Then in the end I stopped drawing."

"So in the head there are scribbles. Is there anything else in other parts of your body?"

"No. It's like before. I only sense something when you ask me to, but it feels like somebody else's body. It's strange. Maybe something has happened to me that I can't remember."

"Do you gain anything by not sensing other parts of your body than your head?" I ask.

"I don't know. What do you think?"

"Well, I think that you don't feel comfort, discomfort, your needs too clearly."

It goes quiet.

"I'm curious," she says.

I don't want to push her, bring anything up too early, don't want to create false memories about something that may not have happened. Yet at the same time the space is so filled with this, it is so obvious now. It's like an invitation, as if she—or a part of her—in many and indirect ways has told me this without saying it openly and plainly, as though she wants me to put words on something wordless.

"I have an idea of what this is about. How do you feel? If it rings true to you, we can explore it. But remember this is just my assumption and I can put it aside. It's only my interpretation and not an objective truth about you."

"I want you to say it."

"Some people have experienced something very painful happen to their body at some point in life, and they then distance themselves from the body."

"It happened when I was five or six years old. It was my aunt's partner who did it. I just went into some sort of freeze, I guess." Nina speaks in the same tone as she used when telling me about the cancer diagnosis, as though this was about a trip to the shop. "Mom said that I either had to report it or stay quiet about it."

So her mother put the responsibility and decision on her—and what a decision: report or stay quiet. Not strange that she can pack things down and hold them in.

"I hear what you are telling me and am moved, Nina. At the same time, I become aware of your tone. It's as though this was about a trip to the shop."

"Well, there's not much to be gained by making a big deal out of it now. My aunt and that guy broke up soon after."

"How is it for you when we talk about this?" I ask.

"I wonder what I've shared with you so that you could have guessed this. I'm worried that others could also guess. I wouldn't have said this to you by myself."

"No. And I am bound by confidentiality, as you know. This is a safe space."

"Yes. Not even my boyfriend knows about this. Only my best friend. I have many secrets."

I'm curious about what other secrets Nina has. Yet as a gestalt therapist I am first and foremost concerned with the phenomenon, how secrecy is experienced for her and myself, not necessarily that the content of the secrets must be exposed here in the therapy room or otherwise.

"You have many secrets. How does that feel for you?"

"Fine."

It goes quiet again. There is much silence between us. It's not just Nina who has secrets, I think to myself. When meeting with clients, as a rule, I keep my own story and experiences to myself unless I think that it might have a therapeutic effect to share something. Still, there are some experiences that I have rarely shared with anyone, and now I wonder if this is also due to shame.

"I don't want this to change your impression of me. I don't want to be seen as weak and in need of help," she says.

"I know that you can also be active and strong."

"Why couldn't I have been angry there and then? That was really the sort of situation where I could have used my anger and asserted myself. I'm a coward."

"I want to tell you something that I have experienced, Nina. The context was very different, and I was an adult, but I have also experienced rape. There are many of us who have experienced sexual abuse in one form or another. After first resisting, I found myself disappearing from my body, going into a freeze." I hear that my voice is shaky. This is difficult for me. But it is important to share, important to share this secret with Nina now.

"At least you tried to resist at first. I didn't even do that," she says.

"Nina, actually I don't think I resisted much. This is so shameful for me too. I think I didn't resist much at all. I went into a freeze reaction. And you were a child, Nina. If there is no help available, and the possibilities for fight or flight are small, freeze can be the best adaptation to danger. It's largely instinctive and not something that we choose."

We continue talking for a while about danger and the typical reactions. I try to normalise this. I feel less shame myself as well.

"Before we conclude, I wonder if we should make a deal about what we have talked about today. Would you rather that we don't continue exploring this episode with your aunt's partner, or do you want to explore this further in the future? You decide."

"I don't need do delve into it, but it's not taboo to bring it up," she says. "If anything comes up and it's relevant, we can go on to explore it."

We meet a few more times. Then I get an email. Nina writes that she's very busy—with cancer treatment, work, and other things—that she needs to wait with therapy. I write that it's precisely now, during such a period, that it might be a good idea to continue with therapy, but that it's her choice. She decides not to come. To respect her decision is good, I think to myself, and I choose not to push her. Yet I wonder if this is happening because I exposed her secret—and maybe my own. Have I done something wrong? Again I feel shame: am I a good enough therapist?

Summer comes. I can't imagine Nina in her black clothes during the light summer months. I don't hear anything from her. Then finally in September, she contacts me again by email and books a new session.

She arrives and greets me, this time without a hug. We sit down, and it's quiet.

"There's a lot going on. I'm tired," she says. "I don't know where to start."

"It's good that you know how you feel, Nina. Do you also know what you would like us to do now that you are tired?"

"I don't know," she replies. "Yes, for you to ask questions."

"Okay. I hear that you say that there's a lot going on. How's it going with your cancer treatment?"

"It's okay."

"Has anything happened between you and your partner?"

"Yes, we broke up. It became too much. He hit. I broke up. I've thought about Angry-Nina and everything else. There's a reason she's here, Angry-Nina."

"Yes, there is a reason she's here."

"He's moved out, but still shows up regularly with various excuses. Yesterday he needed to get some tools for work. He hugged me, for a long time. I told him that it wasn't okay."

"Good, Nina. Good that you feel that it isn't okay for you and that you say so."

"Yes." It's quiet again for a moment before she continues: "Earlier today I sat down on the warm bathroom tiles and cried. That was okay as well."

Something could defreeze, I imagine, on those warm bathroom tiles. This is the first time Nina tells me that she has cried.

"Good that this is okay for you too. You can do something other than pack down and hold in now."

"Yes."

"I've noticed another important change as well, that we didn't hug today," I say.

"That's true."

"And I think that's good as well, Nina, very good. I don't need any hugs, and I know how you feel about it."

"It's strange, Vikram, but it's as though we are closer now that we don't hug."

Nina discovers that she's pregnant. It happened just before they broke up.

"My best friend thinks that I should get an abortion."

Yes, I immediately think, absolutely an abortion. Yet I'm also concerned with what Nina wants, with what is right for her. "And what do you want?"

"I both want and don't want to have the baby."

Maybe we can explore the two poles want and don't want through chair work, but before I can suggest anything Nina continues talking: "When I went to see my doctor, he didn't even want to discuss the possibility of abortion."

"I don't want to advise you one way or the other, Nina, but I think that you should go to another doctor where talking about abortion is possible at least." I say this as calmly as I can while I am furious with this doctor who barely knows Nina, only his own principles. Another instance of abuse, I think to myself.

"Yes. My mother also calls all the time. I haven't told her anything, not about the pregnancy or about the break-up. I screen who's calling before I decide to answer now. I'm talking less with her."

"You're aware of your needs and take care of yourself," I say.

"I don't want to be like my mom and my aunt. I want to be strong. But I don't feel strong. I'm the oldest member of the family, Vikram, older than mom and my aunt." She smiles a little. "I've always been treated like that. Sometimes I've just needed to have a mother."

It strikes me that her mother may have suffered much as well and have an unmet need for a mother herself. These things can stretch across generations. Nevertheless, now it is Nina who is sitting here—and myself. As therapist, I can be like a mother, I think to myself, a little and for a little while.

"This is a safe space. Here we have already made many important experiences together. I suggest an experiment. I want to get that blanket lying on the chair over there and give it to you."

I get up. I want to care for Nina, allow her to be something other than strong, and I know that physical contact doesn't feel like care to her. Hence the blanket.

"How is that for you?" I ask.

It seems like she is going into freeze again.

"How are you feeling, Nina? Check with yourself. We don't need to do this. What's happening with you right now? Any thoughts, feelings, sensations?"

She looks at me. "Immediately I got the idea that you would put the blanket over my head so that I couldn't see, that I would suffocate. It's so absurd."

"Okay, so that's what happened to you. It's great that you could become aware of that. And just to clarify, I meant to put it on your lap. But now I think that I'll simply hand it to you so that you can decide if you want to take it or not. What do you think about that? We can also drop the idea entirely."

"No, it's nice that you give it to me."

I hand the blanket to her, and she takes it and spreads it around herself, the black blanket. "It's so strange that I responded by getting the thoughts that I did," she says.

"Or not so strange. It could be related to previous experiences. I think that it was good that you became aware of what was happening and that we could clarify what I intended to do. Then you could experience the situation here and now differently and as something new."

"Yes." She touches and looks at the blanket she has around her.

We are getting close to the end of our session. I am concerned with what happens after and between the sessions. There are several major life-events happening at the same time for her now. She needs social support, I think to myself, and I'm not mother.

"You have experienced some big changes in your life lately, Nina. You said that you have talked to your best friend. I think that is very good. You also said that you have the need for a mother sometimes. Maybe you can get a little support from your best friend. Maybe you don't need so much advice, just that she and others are with you, simply being together. Check with yourself. Maybe you can tell them what you need."

"Yes," she says and goes quiet a moment. "I don't know if I'm ready to be a mother yet."

Nina has been to another doctor. "It was too late for an abortion anyways, so there's no longer any decision to be made," she tells me.

"I'm weak, Vikram. But now I just have to make this work." Her voice is forced, as though it is pressing past something, different than before.

"I hear you say that you are weak and just have to make it work. I also hear that there is something different with your voice," I say.

"The lump has moved up to my throat, but I don't want to explore it. I must be strong now."

She looks out the window in silence for a long time. I think she is packing down and holding in. But maybe she is choosing this with greater awareness now.

"I notice that you are looking out the window."

"Yes. I don't want to look at you or be looked at. Then the lump will come."

"Okay. I can also look out the window."

It's snowing. Silent. Then, from the corner of my eye, I see some tears in her eyes.

"We mustn't talk about the tears," she says.

"Okay," I say.

Outside the snow is falling softly and in large flakes covering the tree and everything else. Nina probably doesn't see the snow and the tree. She is packing down and holding in. But not only: some tears are falling. Something unfreezes a little. She takes the blanket and spreads it around her. Soon she isn't crying anymore.

We look at each other. "You can also be strong now," I say and smile.

"I hope so." She smiles back at me.

Still, I am also worried for her. There are so many crises at once.

"When will we meet again?" I ask.

"Same time next week?"

"Good." I calm down a little. "What are you doing in the meantime? Are you meeting your best friend?"

"I'm going to meet her this evening. We are just going to hang out and watch a film and eat sweets, I think. That's what I need."

Nina puts down the blanket, and we get up. In the foyer we small talk a little. It seems that she's doing okay.

"I'm going home to just lie down on my sofa a little," she says.

I get an image of her lying on the sofa and have an urge to give her something before she leaves.

"Wait a second."

I get the blanket.

"If you want it?"

"Yes, I do. Thanks, Vikram."

We smile to each other, don't hug, and she goes out the door.

Nina cancels the next session by email. She thanks me for the therapy, but decides to discontinue it. "There's a lot going on. Maybe later," she writes.

Now she must have become a mother.

* * *

Comments on "Freeze"

Freeze: "Freeze" is a physiological and not very conscious reaction found in animals—humans included—to phenomena that are perceived to be dangerous. It can occur when one perceives that a fight or flight reaction is difficult or impossible in the particular situation. Stiffening into a freeze can make the attacker believe that you are already dead and leave you alone, or if the assault happens just the same, the feeling of pain is reduced. Accompanying reactions with many animals include shaking and particular breathing patterns before they apparently return to a normal state.[1] Yet especially with human beings—who have the capacity for various forms of thinking and emotions, both a blessing and a curse in this context—the freeze reaction can later result in shame and post-traumatic stress.[2] In the work with Nina, I associate the freeze reaction with the contact style retroflection.

Therapy with clients who have experienced abuse—differences and similarities: There are some interesting similarities and differences between this story and "Marianne's memories". Often emotional regulation is a theme with seriously traumatised clients. Initially, there was a lot of retroflection with Nina and a lot of expressiveness with Marianne—pole and counter-pole. This was part of the reason for selecting chair work as an experiment with Nina and not with Marianne. Bodily phenomena such as touch are also interesting to compare. While Marianne and I could eventually experience safe touch, it was a victory to stop hugging with Nina. Both situations involved deficient bodily awareness, though expressed in quite opposite manners.

Body work and boundaries: The gestalt therapist Jim Kepner has been interested in the body in therapy.[3] He describes how abuse can involve the abused giving oneself over to the other and an experiencing lack of boundaries, as well as different ways of working therapeutically with this. For example, the experiment where I moved slowly towards Nina and asked her to sense where I should stop was inspired by his work.

Abuse and cancer: Several studies have shown correlations between having been exposed to abuse and degraded mental health. We now also have a number of studies that show that people who have experienced abuse have higher rates of physical disease than others. A Norwegian study from 2007 examined violence and disease among women between eighteen and forty years old.[4] Of those who had been exposed to physical violence, the rate of disease was significantly higher than with the general population. Among those who had also experienced sexual abuse, there were even higher rates. The diseases included asthma, migraines, diabetes, and cancer. According to this and similar studies, this can be due to stress and other common reactions and adaptations following abuse that contribute to an increased vulnerability for developing diseases.

Secrets and secrecy: Secrecy can be a form of retroflection. Especially in these times of social media, exposure, and sharing, it can be important to be reminded that secrecy can have its advantages as well as disadvantages.[5] This can involve putting a boundary up against others. Those who do not share the secret are kept at a distance, while those who share it become more intimate. One then has an inner room where one is in charge, an experience of home, perhaps. In Norwegian the word for secret, "hemmelig", and home, "hjem", are closely related. On the other hand, it may be the case that those who know the secret are not people we have chosen to share it with and be intimate with, an assailant for example. A home is not always safe. In this case, the secret can just as well contribute to maintaining the assailant's power. And often shame is associated with the incident.

In gestalt therapy, it is not a goal in itself for clients to share their secrets with the therapist or others. The only goal is increased awareness; to explore the secrecy as a phenomenon and how it is experienced by the client and others. (A classic experiment is the "I have a secret" game where a client does not actually share the contents of the secret, but instead imagines how others would react if it was shared and how they themselves might feel about it.)[6]

CHAPTER EIGHT

The bearded lady

"Right, what's my name then?"
We're sitting in a circle and are introducing ourselves. The middle-aged person beside me looks at me while asking. Ronny is the name chosen by the parents. Male is the sex that was registered at birth. I remember when I first met Ronny. I saw a slightly balding man, wearing make-up. With large worker's hands he greeted me, nail polish. Indeed, his chest could have been perceived as breasts. My thoughts went immediately to a bachelor party, comical, but involuntarily comical, vulnerable. Ronny also reminded me of a man who lived where I grew up. He often went around in a dress and wearing make-up. Most people thought that he was crazy, and us kids were a little afraid of him. Maybe he was completely sane, and there was something insane about us. Maybe we were the ones who made him crazy.

"Yes, what's your name then?" I ask back.

"Annette. And Ronny. That's what most people call me, but I think I'd rather you all call me Annette here."

"So then you'd also prefer that we use 'she' rather than 'he' as a pronoun for you?" I ask.

"Yes," she replies.

We smile to one another. Tonight Annette is wearing subtle make-up, but is otherwise wearing relatively gender-neutral pants and a T-shirt. This is a small therapy group for transgender individuals held by LLH, the Norwegian association for lesbians, gays, bisexuals and transgender people. I have been asked to facilitate it, and we are to meet a few evenings during the spring in their office in downtown Oslo.

The introduction round continues:

"Hey. My name is Martin. I am in the midst of a female-to-male procedure at Rikshospitalet."

"Harold here. I wasn't so lucky. I was rejected by Rikshospitalet around ten years ago. But as you can see, I've undergone much of the female-to-male procedure anyways. I have had a few operations abroad and I take hormones."

"My name is Lawan. I'm originally from Thailand and underwent a male-to-female procedure there a few years ago."

"My name is Jo. I am registered as male at birth, but feel that my gender identity is fluid. I feel neither like a male or female, so I'd prefer if you used the gender-neutral ze as a pronoun for me."

Soon Annette is talking with the others, smiling and laughing. Already she appears quite relaxed.

"There is something I would like to talk about," she says. "I'm worried about coming out as myself at work."

"Where do you work?" asks Lawan.

"It's a big construction firm."

"And what are you afraid might happen?" continues Lawan.

"I'm afraid of their reaction. And in the worst case I can lose my job. But the transition is starting to be quite apparent. Some of the guys have reacted to me wearing nail polish."

"What do you say then?" asks Jo.

"*They're my own fucking nails. Mind your own business,*" replies Annette while she drums her fingers atop crossed legs.

"How brave of you!" Jo smiles.

"Maybe I can raise this with the HR department," says Annette.

The group continues to explore this possibility together with Annette. She is brave. But, I think, being brave also has something to do with support. Maybe Annette became a bit braver now from Jo's comment. Perhaps *brave* is partly a projection as well, a side that Jo is not so aware of personally, but that ze sees in Annette. Maybe we can support this side in Jo and the others here as well.

"I would like us to explore bravery a little more," I say. "Could you try to say *I am brave*, Jo? Just to see how it feels?"

"I am brave."

"You're laughing," I say.

"Yes. I don't feel brave. Nobody at work knows that I don't only identify as a man," Jo explains.

"So you never wear women's clothes or make-up?" asks Annette.

"Not at work."

"Otherwise?" continues Annette.

"Yes, sometimes."

"Where do you get them from then?" asks Harold.

"The shop."

"So you buy clothes in the women's department? I think that's brave of you."

I am moved. It's beautiful to see Harold get involved and support Jo.

"Oh yeah?" Jo asks.

"It was a big deal the first time I went to buy a suit," explains Harold.

"So maybe you're brave in your own way, Jo? There's a few of us here anyways who think that," I say. "In any case the description *brave* now exists here in this room. I can almost see it as something tangible on the floor within our circle here, something that we are creating together, and there is more than enough for everybody."

The next evening we meet I notice that Jo, who's slim and has medium-length black hair, is wearing a tight-fitting top with a low neckline, likely bought in a women's department. Annette seems to notice as well. She smiles at Jo. We are waiting for Harold, and the group's participants exchange small talk in the meantime. Then he comes in.

"Sorry for coming late. My doorstep is enormous."

"I could see that metaphor very concretely. How enormous is your doorstep, Harold? Can you tell us more about that?" I ask.

"I'm struggling with social anxiety. I'm most often alone at home. I still feel like I don't fit in out there."

Harold continues to explain. I look at him. Few could guess that he, a bearded man, has been anything other than a man, I think. Even so, he feels continual discomfort when he is out among other people. He is careful to play the role of man properly. I get sad thinking about Harold being isolated at home, how society, all of us, contributes to some people not daring to go out their doors.

"Is there anybody else here who recognises this?" I ask.

Several nod. Some share their own experiences.

"So you share the experience of not fitting in," I say after a while. "Thereby everyone somehow fits in here. This is a community."

We take a short break half way through. Some use the break to go to the bathroom. Others make small talk and drink coffee.

"I noticed that there are gender-neutral toilets here," says Jo after the break. "*Everybody* is written on the door. That's great."

A conversation about toilets and changing rooms ensues. I'm struck by the fact that in our society, gender reminders and restrictions are rampant. In Norway, only two genders are recognised socially, medically, and legally. Those who are in between or who experience themselves as a third gender thus become either invisible or extremely visible.

"At the moment I don't know if I should go to the men's or women's changing room when I get changed at my gym," says Annette.

"Maybe you can explain your situation to the people running the gym and see if they have any suggestions, for example a staff changing room while you are going through the transition," suggests Lawan. "That's what I did."

"That's a good idea."

"I also wanted to share something," says Martin. He has been quiet until now. When we met for a private session before the group began, he shared that he has a hard time taking space and that he wanted to challenge himself a little with this. I smile to him and try to communicate support, and I'm curious.

"I had my breasts removed a while ago. Last Saturday I was jogging through the forest. It was so good. The smell of warm pine trees. The sun on my face. So I chose to take off my t-shirt and continue jogging through the forest and spring sun bare-chested. I was so happy that I wanted to scream." Martin smiles while he talks. We all smile.

"That same evening I went to a work party. The men talked about football, acting typically macho, and the women talked about children and make-up and stuff. I first sat with the men, but didn't feel like I belonged. Then I sat with the women, but didn't feel at home there either. I felt so small. Nobody there would have understood me if I had shared my experience from earlier that day. In the end I left."

"So you also choose not to bother pretending that you are interested in football and make-up and stuff like that," I say.

"I guess so, because that doesn't resonate with how I experience myself."

"That's great that you are faithful to your experience of yourself, Martin. And you chose to leave rather than to pretend. There are some limiting social norms, but to a degree we can choose how we relate to them," I say.

"Yes."

"And you choose to come here to this group, and here you share both stories. How does that feel?"

"It feels good. You are the first people I tell these stories to. I feel that I am among people who understand. I feel larger here."

"Now I am moved, Martin. I think that this is an infinitely more beautiful conversation than one about football or make-up."

"Me too," says Jo. "And I recognise the discomfort of not fitting into gender norms."

"Sometimes I can also choose to break with other's expectations. I can, for example, suddenly begin talking about when I was pregnant and about my experiences with that," Harold says, while tugging his beard and smiling. We all smile together.

In addition to social anxiety, an experience of not fitting in and feeling small, these other experiences are now emerging, I think to myself, an experience of choice, to present oneself as one is, to belong in a community of diversity.

After the gathering I walk home with light steps and sense myself smiling. It is a feeling that comes from within and from the ever brighter, warmer evening. I imagine Martin running bare-chested through the forest, Harold with his beard and comments about having been pregnant. I'm also becoming a little braver. A childhood memory pops up: one day a friend of mine laughed at me and said that I wiggled while I walked. I immediately denied this and said that he was the one who did this. Then I became very occupied with walking straight, just right, to not be seen as feminine.

To varying degrees, we can all have traits that don't fit into the dominant gender norms. When we try to conform, we contribute to maintaining these gender norms. We limit ourselves as well as others. Instead of experiencing the whole polarity in ourselves and society, we become rigid and stereotypical. We can become hostile towards the alienated sides of ourselves and we can become hostile towards others who we project these sides upon. This is perhaps experienced most by trans people, a suitable target for projection, but it affects us all. It is important that I now walk with light steps and a smile through Oslo's streets. That I am a man with some movement in my hips is not just liberating for myself, I think to myself, but for us all.

During the course of time that passes between the meetings, Conchita Wurst wins the 2014 Eurovision Song Contest. I'm jubilant. Others' reactions are mixed. "The bearded lady won the Eurovision Song Contest," writes the newspaper *VG* in an editorial under the title *Circus ESC*. "Contestants next year include the giant ape of Borneo and the singing camel." Rage is my first reaction, sorrow my second. There are people who hardly leave their home due to the gender norms. I know this very well. These are people who I am beginning to grow fond of. Fortunately, counter-reactions soon arise to the editorial in other newspapers and media. I write an op-ed myself.

"On time." Harold smiles when we meet the next evening. Maybe his doorstep has become a little smaller—despite *VG*. In any event, he is here right on time. I smile back. Soon the whole group is gathered, and we sit down in our circle.

"I'm unsure if I want to say it," begins Harold. "It might not be very sensitive if others are struggling, but I am feeling really good lately. I know that this feeling will end too, but I am trying to enjoy it right now. And it doesn't hurt that Conchita won."

"Like she says, *We are unstoppable!*" says Jo.

"*We are unstoppable!*" several others yell out in unison. I smile. My eyes well-up.

"I am also quite happy these days," says Jo.

I listen while Jo continues to talk. Meanwhile I notice that Lawan is sitting hunched over and I hear that she is breathing heavily. After a while I turn my attention to her.

"I hear that you are breathing heavily, Lawan, and wonder how you are feeling?"

"It's difficult right now," she replies. "I'm in the middle of a lawsuit with my ex who doesn't want me to have anything to do with our daughter. I'm presented as a freak and an unfit parent." She continues to tell us a little about the difficult conflict. "But we don't need to focus more on me right now."

"You don't want to?" I check.

"No."

"Okay. So this is life, as in this group, something good, something bad, some are happy, some are sad, and everything changing," I say. "Is it okay if we see if others have experiences with children and families?"

Lawan nods.

"When I was in contact with Rikshospitalet, they thought that I should wait with my transition until after my son was 18, or move so that it would not affect him," says Harold. "I chose to let him grow up with my ex-husband and moved to Oslo. They live out on the west coast. We don't have much contact now, but …" He swallows. "I feel that it was necessary and the right thing to do. But of course I miss him."

Maybe it is possible to use an *and* instead of *but*, I wonder. Life is complex. I try: "Yes, it was both necessary and the right thing to do, and at the same time you miss him."

"Yeah, I want it to be okay to miss him even though I myself decided to move, but it's difficult. It's like an abscess that doesn't completely go away. It does feel good to have said something about it here together with you all, though." Harold does something with his shoulders, lifts and then lowers them a little. I think that something has gotten lighter, that it's become a somewhat smaller burden to carry.

"And speaking about fitting in or breaking norms that we talked about last time: my son still calls me mom. It's weird when we are out on the street or with others. Mom … with a beard. But I'm fine with it."

I focus again on Lawan. "And you, Lawan, how do you feel now?"

"I'm breathing," she replies.

We take a break. Harold and Lawan find each other and begin talking. Afterwards in the circle the conversation spontaneously continues on families and partners.

"Luckily I have a lot of support from my parents and siblings," says Lawan.

"My little sister has also been very supportive. It's so touching. And slowly but surely my parents are also beginning to understand," says Martin.

"You're all lucky," says Annette. "My mother doesn't want anything to do with me. My relationship with a woman has also recently ended. She said that she wasn't lesbian. But we are still friends. We are travelling to Brazil together this summer. There I'm going to undergo some gender affirming surgery. I don't know whether I will be attracted to women or if I will eventually be attracted to men. The hormones I take now have taken away my sex drive in any case. How is that for you all?"

"Right now I am actually experiencing a greater sex drive," says Harold. "I think that it's because I'm being more social."

Did he just glance over at Lawan now?

They go out the door together after the meeting.

The next time, Jo shows up in a skirt. It's a Saturday, so ze's probably coming straight from home, I think to myself.

"I see that you're wearing a skirt today, Jo. How does it feel sitting here together with us dressed like that?" I ask.

"It was so nice and warm today, so it feels great."

"And how does it feel sitting with us here and now?"

"I'm happy." Jo smiles. "It feels good to be able to be safe and visible as myself together with you all."

"Is it okay if we ask how the others are feeling?" I ask.

"Yes."

"I'm happy to see you smile like that," says Martin.

"Oh! I'm very happy that somebody else can be happy about this." Jo's smile grows even wider.

"I feel that I should also wear more feminine clothes," says Annette. "That I'm a coward."

Even here, as in all groups, norms and social pressure develop, I think to myself, including those relating to gender and gender expressions. I want to invite Annette to explore if there is a difference between what she feels she should do and what she wants to do.

"Can you try and say *I want to wear more feminine clothes* and see how it feels?"

"I want to wear a skirt." Annette is tasting the words it seems. "Yes, that's true for me," she concludes.

But maybe there isn't enough support for her to feel that she can do that quite yet.

"Also try *I can wear a skirt.*"

"I can wear a skirt." She quickly adds: "No, I can't do that at work and on the underground and outside just yet."

"No, so at work and outside you can't do it yet. How about here?"

"Yes, maybe. I'll think about it."

The conversation continues around different themes. Several members participate. Then we take a short break.

"I would like to express a few thoughts out loud," says Harold when we have all sat down again. The other members smile and nod encouragingly. "It's about my experience with Rikshospitalet. It was ten years ago, but it was a strong experience of not being taken seriously, and of being rejected for who I was. I wonder if I have post-traumatic stress, if I should get an assessment and diagnosis. I have also thought about taking them to court."

For a long time, Rikshospitalet has had a monopoly on assessments and treatments relating to gender identity. Only those who have been diagnosed as transsexual got access to trans-related health services. Many have been rejected. The diagnosis has acted as a judgement, I think to myself, and now, understandably enough, Harold wants to have his case taken up anew and to receive a new judgement. He continues for a while. Then I speak:

"Now you have shared some thoughts. How did that feel?"

"Good."

"And how would it feel to receive feedback from others here? Would you like that?"

"I'm a little afraid that you might trivialise my experience," he replies. "Most people think that post-traumatic stress happens only after rape and war and incidents like that."

Social anxiety is often associated with worries about how people may see us, I think. Through dialogue we can check our worries, but in so doing we risk confirming that they are in fact true.

"Okay. So you can choose to check if we experience it that way, or continue to think that we maybe do so," I say. "I understand and respect your choice either way."

"Yes. No. I do want feedback."

"Okay. Is there anybody who wants to say something about how you are affected by what Harold has told us? I would especially like to invite you to share something about your own bodily sensations and feelings. This is a form of basic information about how we have been affected while he shared his story. It can be more useful than thoughts and evaluations, at least now in the first round."

Lawan starts: "I get angry when I hear how you were treated at Rikshospitalet."

"Personally, I've been fortunate, but it's terrible to see that they're sitting there with such power," says Martin.

"I feel mostly sorrow, I think," says Annette.

"I also wonder if you want to hear what I think about post-traumatic stress, Harold?" I ask.

"Yes, I would," he replies.

"I think that we can experience many other traumas than rape and war. This is also quite recognised among therapists today. And it sounds like the experience you had was very serious for you."

His eyes redden and tears begin to well up.

"We are not Rikshospitalet and we cannot apologise for them," I continue. "We are not doctors or psychiatrists who can diagnose you with post-traumatic stress as a result of your treatment there. Neither are we judges. But we have sat together with you and heard your story, mourned and been angry together with you, Harold."

"Yes. That felt good," he says.

We continue to meet several more evenings. Then one summer day it is our last group session.

"I have something important to share," says Harold. "I have asked my doctor for an examination for post-traumatic stress. And my son had his birthday a few days ago. I was sad to not be together with him. Yet I sense a change: now I let myself feel the sorrow while at the same time I'm okay with having chosen to not be his main caretaker. That's just how life can be."

"Yes, that's how life can be," I repeat.

Lawan is breathing heavily and is sitting hunched over.

"Is it okay if I focus on you a little, Lawan?" I ask. "I hear that you are breathing heavily and see that you are sitting hunched over."

"I am so sick and tired. My own daughter will have her birthday soon, and I am so tired of having to fight for her."

"Yes, you are sick and tired," I repeat. "Just remain with that feeling here, now. Feel your heavy breath. Maybe we can be with you in this for a little while."

I place myself in a similar position and also feel my breathing. We are quiet for a while. Then I hear that her breathing changes and see that she straightens her back.

"What is happening now?" I ask.

"When you paid attention to me, I got to say something about how I felt. And when you simply let me be depressed, something new happened. Otherwise I probably would have simply kept it inside. Out of consideration to the others sitting here. I am quite occupied with everybody else's well-being."

"I think that it's brave of you to fight for your daughter," says Annette.

Her intentions are good, I think to myself, but does Lawan really want evaluations like *brave* right now?

"Would you like feedback now, Lawan?"

"I don't know. If anybody wants to say something, go ahead."

"Now I asked what you want. What happens when I ask you about that?"

"What I want? I want to be in the sun and feel it on my skin, Vikram, to walk in the forest and bathe in the sea, to be with other people, be myself and forget about myself," she says. "But I am constantly reminded that I am trans, different than others, and must fight."

"Yes," I say.

"Could we maybe take a little break? I have brought some food for everyone," she continues after a moment of silence.

"How thoughtful, Lawan. Sure, why not?" I look to the others. Everybody nods and smiles.

Lawan takes out some containers with Thai dishes that she has prepared. We sit down at a table and eat together. What we are doing now is important, I think to myself, almost akin to a ritual. Sharing food is about accepting one another wholly and completely. It is an intimate and loving act. While we eat, a few continue talking about families and children. It is almost like some form of birthday party, I suddenly think. The children are not here, but they are named. Harold talks about his son, Thomas. Lawan talks about her daughter Sirikit. We all share in their stories. This group is also a form of family. Or it has been a family. The meal is also a concluding ritual. Maybe the experiences from the evenings together can also become something bodily, which we carry with us onwards. Like the Last Supper. Jesus may have been trans, I guess. I cast a glance at the clock.

"Thanks for the food, Lawan," I say. "Now I suggest that we gather in a circle again."

"Just start without me. I need to take a trip to the bathroom first." Annette gets up and leaves. The rest of us sit down in a circle.

"Now this group is coming to a close. Does anybody want to say something more about the experiences you have had with the group?" I ask. "What we've accomplished? What we haven't accomplished? What you will take with you from here?"

"I think that this has been good social training for me," says Harold. "I probably should have been out more in the sun this summer. But if I hadn't come here, I probably wouldn't have made it over the doorstep and gotten any sun at all."

"I usually feel so small and have bad self-esteem." While Martin speaks he shows with his fingers just how small he often feels, and I mirror with my own fingers. "But here I have expressed myself and have had a place. Here I feel that I have become larger."

"And how large are you right now?" I ask, still mirroring with my fingers.

Just then Annette returns. She has changed to a dress. "Yeah, just how large are you right now, Martin?" she asks and spins around, then lifts one foot up behind herself. We all laugh. The sexual innuendo is all too obvious.

When the laughter stops, Martin throws his arms out to the side. "Large. I'm large. We are large."

Then everybody turns their gaze towards Annette again.

"So I see that you have changed to a dress, Annette," I say.

She smiles. She has also done something with her hair. Annette is beautiful, and it is more than her physical appearance alone.

"You are beautiful," I continue.

"Thank you."

"Yes, you are beautiful," says Jo.

"How does it feel sitting here together with us dressed like that, hearing this, and being seen in this way, Annette?" I ask.

"Very good. It means a lot for me," she says. "There is something else as well. Yesterday I brought up the changing room issue with the receptionist at the gym. She said that she needed to talk to her manager, but she was sure that they would find a solution. It felt good to be met like this. And I have also had a meeting with the HR person at work. We agreed to find a time to bring this up with all of the employees. I feel that I have his support."

The other group members cheer spontaneously. I am happy that there are some supportive people out there in society. Change that occurs in the therapy room is not sustainable if society constantly requires a different way of being. Fortunately, Norway is undergoing change, I think.

"Now there are only a few minutes left. How would you all like to conclude?" I ask.

"We can exchange telephone numbers and continue to have contact," Jo suggests and looks around. The others smile and nod.

"I would like to give each and every one of you a hug, if that's okay," says Annette.

Everybody gets up and goes around hugging one another. For a moment I'm unsure, but then I get up as well.

"A hug, Vikram?" asks Annette.

"I would like that," I reply.

And so the group dissolves. Lawan and Harold again leave together. I remain a while and clean the room. It is over. Just the vague sensation of the hug against my cheek. When I again walk home with light steps through Oslo's summer evening, I carry with me the image of Annette spinning around in her dress, smiling and radiant.

* * *

Comments on *"The bearded lady"*

Transgender people's situation in Norway: Transgender people share an experience of not entirely fitting into and identifying with the gender that they have been assigned at birth. Gestalt therapy is concerned with contact, and the greater situation and context the client is a part of. This story highlights the importance of attitudes and actions in close relationships as well as in society in general.

Ignorance, negative attitudes, discrimination and harassment of transgender people is widespread in all arenas in Norwegian society, something that affects many negatively.[1] Furthermore, there is not sufficient trans-competence among healthcare professionals, and there are many more than the few diagnosed with transsexualism, who have the need for trans-related healthcare.

Fortunately, there have been a few positive developments. In the spring of 2015, the health minister Bent Høie ordered an investigation of the conditions for changing the legal/official recognition of one's gender in various documents and the organisation of trans-related health services.[2] Key proposals included improved healthcare services, removing the castration requirement in order to change one's legal/official gender—a practice that is likely in conflict with basic human rights—and to closer examine implementation of a third gender option. In the summer of 2015, during Oslo Pride, the health minister announced to a jubilant crowd that the government proposed that a person's own experience of gender should now be the criteria for legal/official recognition of gender.[3]

Gestalt therapy, gender identity, and transgender people: In my work with transgender people, I have seen that gestalt therapy can have a lot to offer.[4] An aware, dialogical approach involves mirroring and validating people as they experience themselves and respecting their subjective truths. In this story this is shown by the respectful use of the name and pronoun that people themselves prefer. Furthermore, polarity theory fits well with the new paradigm within trans-health, where gender is seen as a continuum and sometimes as fluid. In terms of contact styles there are always many that can occur. Gender norms can especially be understood in relation to introjection. Retroflection, projection, confluence and differentiation have also been apparent in the groups that I have facilitated, as was the case in this story as well.

Group therapy: Professor in psychiatry and existential therapist Irvin Yalom has written a classic on group therapy.[5] In this, several advantages of group therapy are highlighted. In this story it becomes clear how clients experience that certain feelings and phenomena are in fact normal and acceptable, that they can give and receive support, exchange information, and experiment with new behaviour in a safe setting and receive feedback. There is also now a lot of good gestalt literature about how we can use an aware, dialogical approach in groups and larger systems.[6]

Gender norms, power, and liberation: Few people—if any—fit fully into the dominant gender norms. That women have historically been oppressed by such norms is clear. That these norms can affect sexual minorities and transgender people is also clear. Yet gender norms even limit heterosexual men. One example of this is the norm "big boys don't cry" from the story "Inside the walls". There are certain groups in society that are more oppressed than others and that have an experience of less freedom when met with dominant norms. At the same time we are all—albeit to varying degrees—exercisers of power as well as subject to power. Each time we allow ourselves to be limited in our gender expression we limit not only ourselves but also contribute to strengthening social pressure and dominant norms. Some queer activists have focused on this, and on liberation regarding gender and sexuality for us all.[7]

CHAPTER NINE

The empty chair

Ask looks me in the eye as he speaks. He has green eyes and a northern Norwegian dialect. His hometown was Tromsø, I think. He wrote something about that when he first contacted me by email, after reading the interview with me on gaysir.no.

He smiles. "I imagine that you got a lot of new clients from that interview. You had a lot of sensible things to say. A nice photo too."

"Thanks."

I can't be attracted. Or? Becoming aware of attraction should be okay. I want to kiss Ask, those lips, be closer to him. But I won't. I'm his therapist. Besides, I already have a partner, Antoine. Ask knows this as well. I mentioned something about it in the Gaysir interview.

"It was also on Gaysir that I met my first boyfriend, Bastian, seven years ago," he says. "I was still in the closet back then. We were together for a few months. Then, on a vacation in Rome, I met Giulio and really fell in love."

Giulio, he may look a little like me.

"I found it difficult. I didn't answer Bastian's calls and finally broke up with a text message."

Ouch, I think. Ask goes quiet. Did he hear that?

"A few weeks later I received a phone call from his mother. Bastian was dead. He had committed suicide. She was really angry and depressed. She said that he took his life because of me."

She needed to manage this in one way or another, I think, something almost unmanageable. Still, how awful that Ask became the scapegoat.

"A few weeks later she called again. She had found a letter from Bastian. She said that I was not to blame. She read the letter to me. Apologised. But I continued to feel guilt and shame. I broke up with a text message. A few words then send. And then Bastian took his life a few weeks later. I wasn't sure whether I should continue with Giulio, but in the end decided to stay with him. Rome was exciting, and Giulio really wanted to take care of me. But I also wanted to work and have an everyday life in Norway, and Giulio didn't want to move here. It ended up with us seeing each other during long weekends and holidays. We had a lot of good times, but …"

So similar to Antoine and me, I think.

"Lately I've felt that it's just getting worse and worse between us," Ask continues. "We don't communicate well. I'm fairly quiet, and hold a lot back while Giulio is more expressive and rather direct."

Again how similar to Antoine and me, but reversed. I am Giulio.

"He can get quite jealous, actually. *Have you been a puttano? Whose cazzo have you sucked tonight?* He can say things like that after I've been out for a drink."

I feel sorry for Ask. Giulio sounds fierce. I'm not that bad. Still, the subtexts beneath our harsh words are often: Do you love me, am I good enough, are you going to leave me for another? And uncertainty and a need for control are even more understandable when a relationship begins with infidelity.

"I've actually never been sexually unfaithful. But I have looked at other men."

I've become a priest who is receiving confession. But I could just as well have been the one giving confession. There is an attraction between us, therapist and client, and there are several parallels between what he is telling me and my own life. There are a lot of things I need to work with here—also in order to be a good therapist for him. I need to contact my supervisor afterwards. Yes, I'll do that. Already I notice that I can put myself a little to the side and see and hear Ask more clearly.

"And then it happened. A month ago I got drunk in a bar and went home with a guy. When I talked with Giulio a few days later, he had a whole tirade of questions, found out about it and broke up with me."

Ask often holds back, and Giulio is *rather direct* as he called it. This is something they do together, this way of being in contact. At the same time Ask has a certain responsibility for his contribution to it. Holding back could also be a form of emotional unfaithfulness, and maybe his one-night stand was an indirect way of breaking up. Should I say something about this? No, not now anyway. Here and now with me he is doing something other than holding back. Maybe this is what he needs now.

"But then a few days ago he said that he wanted to fix things, that I should come to Rome, that there's something *pathological* in me that I need to work on. He uses words like that. He's a doctor. But it's over. That's what I want."

"It's over. That's what you want," I repeat. "Have you said this directly to him?"

"I'm not sure," he replies.

Ask continues to share his story and feelings with me. They still talk regularly by phone and Skype. How clear is it for Giulio that things are over, that Ask has made his decision? How clear is this for Ask himself?

"I've created a profile on Grindr—you know, that dating app—and texted a little with a guy there, but we haven't met physically. I thought that I would feel free, but I also feel a loss. I've lost weight and feel an anxiety in my body. I find it difficult concentrating at work and I have started drinking too much in the evenings. Sometimes I wonder if I should go to Rome to be together with Giulio, to make it work. But mostly I'm in a place where I just want to close all of the windows and doors. I'm a little afraid of falling back to how it was when I was in the closet, that I hide and close myself up."

It goes quiet.

"I've listened to you, Ask, and think that I got most of what you told me. I have heard that you were in the closet and were together with Bastian. Then you fell in love with Giulio. It was difficult, and you broke up with Bastian in the end with a text message. He later took his own life. His mother accused you and you felt guilty, but then she apologised and said that it wasn't your fault. Giulio and you have had good times but also difficulties together. There is distance both geographically speaking as well as in the manner in which you communicate. One evening you got drunk and went home with a guy. Now it may be over with Giulio, and at the same time you feel a loss. Is this right? Have I understood correctly?"

"Yes."

"And how does that feel?"

"It feels good."

"In this relationship here and now with me, you are doing something other than what you have done with Giulio or when you were in the closet. You aren't holding back, instead you're sharing and being open. This is another type of relationship, less characterised by conflict for example, so it is far from the same, but I think that this experience may be valuable in itself."

Ask's cheeks redden somewhat. "Yes," he says.

"We are nearing the end of this session. Do you have any questions for me, about gestalt therapy, about me as a person or anything else?"

"I realised that in the Gaysir interview you mentioned that your partner lives abroad. So maybe you have some experiences that resemble my own?"

I smile. "I have experience with long distance relationships, sure. The dynamic with one who is direct and another who holds more back is also something I'm familiar with, both personally and professionally."

"I feel that I'm really seen and heard with you, Vikram, and would like us to continue with therapy."

"I would be happy to continue with you too, but—speaking of distance—it might be difficult with you living in Tromsø and me here in Oslo. One possibility is for me to refer you to a therapist who lives in the same city as you. Or we could try Skype and you coming here whenever possible, but this is not ideal."

"I understand, but I would prefer to continue with you."

"Okay," I say, and I'm glad.

We stand up. He extends a hand. Ask's hand. Afterwards I book an appointment with my supervisor. Then in the evening I skype Antoine. The connection is bad. It's frustrating and the conversation is not a very good one. I look forward to seeing Ask again, those green eyes, his lips, to hear his voice, him saying my name.

Through his laptop's camera he shows me around his flat in Tromsø. This is how Ask lives, I think. A family photograph. A few plants. Through the window I can see the fjord and the mountains.

"I've felt a lot better after our last session," he says. "I've gotten out more. Drunk less. Gotten the urge to exercise more too." He is wearing a white T-shirt. Contrasting with the white shirt is his bare skin—already browner from the spring sun—biceps and veins. Occasionally I look at the little image of myself included in the lower corner of my screen. This is how I appear through the camera. Maybe I should go to the gym afterwards.

"But then Giulio called again yesterday. It was a tiring two-hour conversation. Monologue rather. Afterwards I felt anxious, drank a few glasses again in the evening and slept badly." He smiles faintly. I see now while he continues to talk about their conversation that his green eyes also have a little redness and tiredness in them.

"I wonder if you want to explore this more here and now?" I give some details about chair work.

"Yeah, we can try that," he says, getting up and placing two chairs to face each other and so that they are visible to the camera. He sits in one chair.

"There you are yourself?"

"Yes."

"Can you imagine Giulio in the empty chair? Can you describe him a little?"

"He has dark hair and brown eyes. He is tall. Fit. Handsome. But right now it's like there is only a bunch of words. There are just a bunch of words and arm gestures."

"And you, what are you feeling? What are you doing?"

"Nothing. I don't know."

It goes quiet a moment. Apparently, I think. For according to Ask, there is a bunch of words coming from the other chair. Maybe it can help to place them there.

"Do you want to try to sit a little as Giulio, to talk from there, to make clearer all of the words and gestures?"

He nods, gets up and sits down in the other chair.

"I should have known you would do this to me one day. What will your family think now? Yet another stronzo homosexual. And what about my mother? You know how much she cares about you. But I am still willing to give you a chance, not that you deserve one."

He goes on like this, without stop, for several minutes. Shut up, I think to myself, but I don't say anything. It's important that I'm here as a witness, but right now I believe that Ask also needs some more active support.

"Okay. See if you can now sit down as yourself again."

He switches chairs and goes quiet again.

"I heard a lot when you played Giulio in the other chair, a lot of feelings and words. When you sit as yourself, I hear nothing. Can you tell me something about what is happening with you when you sit there now?"

"Well. This is what I feel, that our communication is bad, that when I try to say something it is not heard or it is misunderstood. Or maybe I'm just bad at communicating."

"Can you imagine Giulio in the other chair and say that directly to him, what you just said to me?"

"Perhaps I don't say enough. It's my fault."

"And the other thing you said to me. That when you try to say something you are not heard or are misunderstood. Maybe try to say it with some of the power you had when you spoke from Giulio's chair. I believe you also have some power within you. Maybe try standing while you say it."

Ask stands up. "You don't hear me." His voice is louder. "You misunderstand. Our communication is not working."

"Good! How was that?"

"Yeah, it felt right. And good. I also feel stronger myself."

"Are you done, or do you want to try to sit as Giulio again and see what happens more?"

He sits down in Giulio's chair. "You're a puttano and I should dump you. You will never find someone like me, with such looks, education, and job. You are lucky. You should think about all the pain you have caused me. You've already killed one ex."

Then it goes quiet. *You've already killed one ex* is left hanging in the air.

"I think that you need to move over to your chair again now," I say.

Ask moves again, slowly. He sits silently, for a long while.

"What is happening with you there? I see that you are sitting a little hunched over."

"I feel a heavy burden."

"Okay. Can you get up from the chair now and shake it all off a little? And then you can put away the chairs and sit in front of the camera again."

He does this.

"What do you feel and think yourself after this chair work?" I ask.

"I feel like I'm a bad person. That I have been silent and held back. That I should have participated in another way. Shown how I felt and what I wanted. And then there's the sexual aspect and unfaithfulness. And the thing with Bastian comes up again."

"That you killed him?"

"Yes."

Has he swallowed this message whole? Maybe we can chew on it a little together?

"Do you yourself believe that you killed him?"

"No, but I did affect him and contribute to it in one way or another. I could have done something differently. Communicated in a different way with him as well."

I get an urge to try to convince him that of course it wasn't his fault, to be Ask's defence, free him from this terrible feeling. But then at one point while I listen to him speaking, it strikes me that guilt may be experienced as important to him. And it is important that I respect that.

"Okay," I say. "I think that there is a difference between guilt and shame. I wonder if some of the shame, the feeling that you are a bad person, can be translated into guilt, that you have done something wrong, something you could have done differently like you say. Is there something you have done, something you feel that you are guilty of, with Bastian, Giulio or somebody else that you think you can take responsibility for and make up for now?"

"I have held back feelings and shied away from conflicts with Giulio. Maybe because I have been afraid of losing him. And then it has culminated and in the end it's me who wants to get away from him, and he doesn't understand anything, he hasn't been given the opportunity to relate to me and the way I have actually felt."

"Can you make this right somehow now?"

"In future relationships I will be more honest and open about how I feel."

Future relationships. So it is over, him and Giulio? Maybe they have come as far as they could together.

"Okay. That's an intention?" I ask.

"Yes. A sort of promise maybe," he replies.

"So when you promise this, you can be freed from the guilt?"

"Maybe."

Perhaps a ritual of this sort, where I almost play the role of a priest granting absolution after Ask promises to be more open, can work. But this too, this counter-pole, can also become a fixation, I think, that now he has to be honest and open and express his feelings all of the time. I want to say something about this.

"I think that these are different ways of being in contact, Ask, to be open and to hold back. And the one is not absolutely good and the other absolutely bad, it depends on the situation. You can hold back, and this can be right in certain situations. I, for one, still have something to learn there. And yet I hear that you want to develop the counter-pole more."

"Yes, I don't want to hold back important things and be so afraid of conflicts." He goes quiet for a moment. "But I guess I'm afraid of being too direct and of what might happen."

I nod. "I can understand that. If you hold back in our sessions, let's just explore it as a phenomenon rather than a problem. At the same time I invite you to follow through with your promise with me as well, to be honest and direct. I can handle it. In therapy you can try out something new."

And I think to myself: it's not going to kill me, Ask.

"I still haven't ended it clearly with Giulio. It's difficult. I still have feelings for him. And I don't want to be alone. I want it to be over, and I want it to continue."

It's not simply guilt and fear for what might happen with Giulio that's keeping Ask in the relationship. Maybe chair work can illuminate further the part of him that wants it to be over and the part that wants to continue with the relationship.

"It's like I'm in a room with lots of doors," he continues.

That was an interesting image, *a room with many doors*. Maybe a guided fantasy instead?

"If you want, we can explore this room more through a guided fantasy."

"That sounds exciting."

"Okay. Then you can close your eyes or rest your gaze in front of you," I begin. "Imagine that you are now standing in the middle of this room with many doors. Become aware of the room, how it feels here, whether you are standing alone or together with somebody else. Imagine the different doors as well. How do they look? What might be behind these doors? Maybe you can't completely know what lies behind them. If you choose a door—when you choose—you forego the other opportunities. How does that feel? What is your impulse and how do you act?"

I let it be quiet a moment before I lead him out of the guided fantasy. "Now you can sense your breath, the chair and the floor, and open your eyes when you are ready."

I see Ask open his eyes and look at me through the camera, again those green eyes.

"There were openings and roads to Rome, Tromsø, the mountains, different places," he recounts. "And Giulio was in a way in the room together with me. He floated a little above me so that I could pull him down if I wanted. It felt both good and confusing. It's strange, but I actually wanted to ask Giulio for advice about where I should go."

"I can understand that," I say. "A decision can involve uncertainty, loss, sorrow over the loss, a responsibility. There is an existential weight to this. It's often easier to let others decide than to feel yourself what you want and take responsibility and choose. And it appears that getting Giulio's advice and input has been something that has characterised much of your relationship."

While I talk I see that occasionally Ask bites his lower lip. Perhaps he is also biting his tongue. Is he holding something back from me now, irritation or something else? I don't know. It's sexy in any case. I hear my own voice, a lot, and soon realise that I'm sharing much of my own story, about Antoine and me. Am I sharing a bit too much now?

"Now I hear myself talking and talking, Ask. What is happening with you?" I ask.

He smiles. "I think that it's interesting."

"Okay."

"And I got an urge to try going back into that room one more time," he says.

I smile and nod. He closes his eyes. "I'm going down a corridor now. Going alone." He continues without encouragement to describe what is happening, so that I too follow along on his journey. I don't choose for him. I don't even guide him now. But he is not completely alone, because he is telling and I am listening.

"I come to a room. There is a sofa in the middle. I sit down. And then another person comes. He sits beside me. We are lovers. I don't know who it is, only that we are lovers. We know each other well. We just sit here together. I feel a peace. And we both want to go on together. We stand up and move towards an opening, a light, towards an open and magnificent sky, out into the mountains."

Ask opens his eyes and looks at me.

"So a change occurred there," I say. "First you walked alone. Then you met a lover, sat with him, and went onwards together. How does it feel in your body and otherwise now?"

"It feels good. I feel tingling in my legs. Like after a workout."

"And is this somehow meaningful in your life at the moment? Is there something you can take from this? Something you get an urge to do?"

"Yes, I need to make it clear that it's over with Giulio in order to move on." Then he goes quiet again. Ask goes silent sometimes. My impulse is to talk, but I hold back now, with awareness. Eventually he comes with more words.

"It's just the matter of closing the door behind me. I feel a loss and am still a little in that other image, where Giulio is and I can choose to go on together with him."

"Yes, you are in the midst of a decision now," I say. "It can involve loss and sorrow. It's only by acknowledging this, and by giving space to the sorrow, that you can truly move on."

We begin to wrap up the session. Ask is taking a summer holiday with his family, so it will be some weeks till next time. A few days later I meet my supervisor. Then I too take a holiday, together with Antoine.

Ask is sitting summer tanned before me in my therapy room in Oslo again. We small talk about our holidays, about what he has done and what I have done. He is handsome, but I'm no longer so attracted. Fortunately. I have held back, managed to listen and see and become more familiar with him as a whole person. I have acknowledged and explored the attraction both on my own and during supervision. It feels like it has moved on to a love that is appropriate to the therapeutic room. While attraction may partially be due to the unknown and projection, love involves seeing the whole other person more clearly as well as myself. Good therapy is love. The fact that I have spent time together with Antoine this summer has also been important, I think, that we have nurtured our love. This does something to my relationship with Ask as well.

"By the way, I called Giulio after our last session," he tells me. "It was tough, but it felt right. And I managed to shoot in a few words."

Shoot in. That's fitting, I think, when the metaphor for conversation is war.

"It's over now."

"And you have shot in those words. You have managed to be direct with Giulio."

"Yes. He still sends some emails, and I send brief replies. That's fine. They're usually not very pleasant, but then at least I know that he's alive."

Ask has been more direct, but it's a fine balance, because *you've already killed one ex*. And he still has feelings for Giulio.

"Others around me are mostly happy that it's over. They are angry at Giulio for the way he has behaved towards me, but I don't feel that way. We've also had many good times. That was why it was so hard to end it completely."

"Yes. And here you also give space to these feelings. You can both assert yourself and be direct, and you can have good thoughts and feelings for him. How does this feel?"

"It feels good to be able to give space to all of this here together with you, Vikram. I couldn't do this with my family and friends this summer," he says. "Oh, there's one other thing I have to tell you: I've met that guy, Nikolai, a few times. You know, the one from Grindr. I've mentioned him before, right?"

I nod.

"We'll see," he says.

We continue therapy throughout the autumn. Occasionally we meet in person, but most often we meet via Skype. Ask is in Tromsø. Sometimes I'm in Oslo, other times at Antoine's. Ask is feeling better, sleeps well, drinks less, exercises, feels less anxious and is able to concentrate at work. He seems to be slowly freeing himself from the guilt. It seems he is keeping his promise. He is more open and direct with his family, friends, and colleagues. He also lets me know if he disagrees with something I say or do. With Nikolai it is mostly first-love and conflict-free for the time being. During the course of the autumn they move in together.

Antoine and I also agree to move in together. We did have a great time when we were together those summer weeks—by and large. And if we are to have a future together, we can't continue living with this distance between us. I decide to move. I feel loss and sorrow as well as happiness. I make plans to shut down my practice in Oslo before next summer and notify my clients already now. In spite of this—or perhaps because of this—the conflicts between Antoine and me increase. I get loud and expressive; he gets quiet and hangs up or walks away.

More and more my sessions with my supervisor begin to resemble therapy. He was in fact once my therapist. And I can't handle starting with a new therapist now, there's already enough changes. We agree to end the supervision relationship so that he can be my therapist again. I'll find another supervisor.

Together we explore what is happening between Antoine and me. Calm and silence have long been a favourite projection and a side I've been less aware of in myself. This probably constituted at least a part of my infatuation with Antoine—and maybe with Ask as well. Over time—as is so common with couples—this has become a strong and painful polarisation between us, especially when we are in conflict: I become more pushy and emotionally expressive when Antoine holds back or isolates himself—and vice versa in a sort of vicious circle. My therapist and I place some chairs on the floor. When I sit in Antoine's chair, something happens with me. I grow afraid. I also remember something he has told me, that it was dangerous to express feelings when he grew up. Together maybe we can now grow in love and be healed. Maybe we can expand our repertoire, I can hold back and he can open up and express his feelings more. At the least, we can better understand each other's ways of being in contact.

Sometimes we do experience this, Antoine and I can be in contact in slightly different ways, even when we are in conflict. Still, I don't know if it's sufficient.

"I don't think that we'll be in touch by email any longer now," Ask tells me during a session. "Last week I received an email from Giulio where he wrote that he had found a tumour. I got the impression that he was dying. I called him several times until I got a hold of him. He asked me about Nikolai. I had mentioned him in a previous email. I don't know if that was smart, but I didn't want to keep it a secret either. When we talked on the phone, he asked more about him, and I told him a little. Then he said *you've done enough damage to my health* and that from that point on he didn't want to have any more contact. He concluded with *vaffanculo*."

Ask smiles. "At least I got the impression that he wasn't dying after all."

"Yes."

"And it's probably best that we don't have contact any longer," he continues. "At the same time I care for him. Giulio is not well."

Maybe it's possible to feel this care—to even express it—and at the same time let go, I wonder.

"If you want, we can try a sort of meditation where you can wish yourself, Giulio and others well." I explain about metta.

Ask wants to try, and I guide us through the meditation.

"Now you can imagine that someone you care for is sitting here in front of you and wish this person well."

I think about Antoine. May you be safe, Antoine. May you have good health. May you be happy. May you be free.

I don't know who Ask is imagining. Maybe it's Giulio. Or maybe it's Nikolai. Maybe somebody else.

"And now somebody you have a more difficult relationship to," I continue.

Giulio—Ask's version of him, or rather my version of Ask's version—is the first thing I think of now. I have probably projected some of my own shadow sides onto him, sides that I have thought that I shouldn't have: uncertainty, jealousy, rage, fierce expressions. So now when I wish you well, Giulio, wish you well exactly as you are, I am also healed a little.

"Just sit a moment and be aware of how you feel here and now," I say. "When you are ready, you can open your eyes."

I open mine. I see tears in Ask's green eyes. He says nothing. We let it be silent. Just the occasional strange, electronic Skype noises from time to time.

The first snow has begun to fall in the north. Ask shows me through his camera. Then he sits down facing me. Serious.

"Nikolai and I have had a conflict."

The summer of love is over, I think.

"Or, that's the thing. I don't know if it even was a proper conflict," Ask continues. "I had a long day at work last Friday, and then I had to hurry and buy groceries and pick up Nikolai from his job. From there we were going to drive and pick up a friend of his at a hotel. I got lost, and Nikolai began saying things like *you're from this town and you can't even find your way around*. I just kept on driving. Didn't say anything. When we got home, they sat down and chatted while I began to cook dinner. My cooking must have been different than what Nikolai had in mind. *Is that how you're going to do it? This is just a mess.* Or something like that. I felt that I was getting irritated, but then I thought that it was better to just finish the food. That was probably a bad idea."

"I don't know. I've also found that it's often a good idea to eat first," I say and smile.

"Yes, but I didn't bring it up with him later either. And now I'm afraid that these things will build up, my irritation and frustration."

"Okay. Maybe you would like to explore this more here and now?"
He nods.

"You can close your eyes or rest your gaze in front of you," I begin. "Take a moment to simply be aware of your body from within. Maybe recall the situation in the car or when you were cooking dinner. *You're from this town and you can't even find your way around.* Pay attention to your body. *Is that how you're going to do it? This is just a mess.*"

"I notice a sensation in my legs," he says. "Muscles tensing."

Didn't Ask become aware of his legs after the guided fantasy in the beginning of the therapy as well? A tingling, as though he had just been to the gym? This can be an important body part, one of the places where it can *build up*, as he calls it, one of the places where he can hold himself back. Maybe he can become even more aware of this as something he does himself, that it's not simply *muscles tensing*, something that happens to him.

"So you tense your leg muscles?"

"Yes, I do."

"Continue to be present with this. Tense the muscles. Sense yourself doing this. Just see what happens."

"Now it's suddenly more a sensation of energy, motion, kicking wildly. I get the urge to stand up."

"Maybe you can do that."

He gets up and moves around. "I feel a little stupid, but wow! It's so good, Vikram." Through the camera I can only see the lower part of his arms, the middle of his body, a little of his legs in motion. Ask laughs. I laugh too.

Then, after a while, he sits down again.

"So, now you have felt even more of this polarity in you, bodily as well. If you want, we can further explore it using chair work. See if we can also put some words on this. What do you think?"

"Yes, I want to." He gets two chairs and sits down in one of them. "Here I am control. In the other chair is the power I felt."

"Okay."

I am an observer. Ask knows the principles behind chair work now. He switches between the two chairs and talks from both sides so there is a dialogue:

"You get so out of control, you explode and are just destructive."

"If you respect me, then I respect you. I also have a potential that can be used for something good."

"But those times when you have come out have turned into explosions. Can you come out a little more gradually?"

"I will try."

It goes quiet.

"Do you feel finished?" I ask. "Should we share some observations and reflections together?"

"Yes." He clears away the chairs and sits down facing the camera again. "The power is something I can use more often, something I want to use more. I remember something that you said about this a while back, Vikram. That the power I played out in Giulio's chair was also something that I had within me."

"Yes. Otherwise I doubt you would have been able to play his role so well. But we often alienate certain sides of ourselves, project them onto others or relegate them to a part of the body that we become less aware of."

"Yes, I experience both my power and my self-control as something that resides in my body. I feel it especially in my legs."

"So maybe now it will be easier to put your foot down. Both physically and metaphorically." I smile.

"Yes. I will express myself to Nikolai and others with clarity and power, but in a decent manner. It doesn't need to be dangerous. There doesn't need to be an explosion."

Ask and I continue working on each of our poles and for the most part in different rooms, but what we have in common is that both are getting quicker at becoming aware of irritation, frustration, and other emotions, also bodily, and that we can choose what we do with them: Ask shares his feelings and asserts himself with Nikolai, I hold back a little longer and consider a moment before I choose how I will express myself with Antoine.

"Now you should probably stop seeing Vikram, Nikolai said the other day," he says one session. It sounds like a new demand, not so unlike the dynamic with Giulio. How will Ask respond to this?

"Now you should probably stop seeing Vikram," I repeat.

"Yes, that's what he thinks, but I don't want that. I want to continue."

"Do you tell Nikolai this as well?"

"I will tell him." Ask goes quiet a moment. "He probably thinks that we are talking about him and me, the problems that we have, or about Giulio. The fact that I still come to you must mean that I think there are problems in our relationship, or that Giulio is still a part of my life. But our sessions aren't only about Giulio or Nikolai."

"No."

We have a few sessions after this, but then a long time passes where I don't hear anything from Ask. Maybe it's because of Nikolai. Maybe Ask is holding himself back after all. Or maybe he doesn't feel the need for therapy. After all there have been a lot of changes in his life.

This spring means endings for me. I prepare for the move. I conclude therapy with several clients. It moves me. As a gestalt therapist, I have let myself be affected. For a moment I wonder if it is mostly due to my own needs, but I don't hold back; I send a text message:

> Hi Ask! It has been a while since the last time we talked, and as you know I'm planning on moving. I would like to know if you want to book a new appointment. Even if you don't feel like you need more therapy now, a closing session can be important. It can, among other things, lead to new experiences with ending relationships. But in the end it's your decision.

I quickly get a reply:

> Hi Vikram! I was just thinking about you yesterday. I'm actually in Oslo on Friday. Would that work?

Ask thought about me yesterday. I smile. Antoine is arriving on Friday afternoon, but I'll probably have time for a therapy session in the morning. I text a confirmation to Ask.

"Sorry that I've been so quiet," he says when we meet. "How long has it been?"

"A few months maybe?"

"Oh. It doesn't feel like it, probably because I often think about you and the work we've done together."

Ask thinks about me. He thinks about us. I'm glad.

"How have you been since we last met?" he asks.

"As you know, I've decided to move so that Antoine and I can live together. Lately I've spent a lot of time wrapping things up. It can be painful at times, I feel, but it's important nonetheless. I also wanted to talk with you about this."

"Yes."

"I'm happy to continue the therapy with you by Skype, but it will become even more difficult to meet in person after I move."

"Yes. I guess it will be more difficult," he says. "But I'm sure it will be good for the two of you to finally live together."

"Different in any case," I say.

"It's a little ironic. It has been a year since we began. Then, I was in the middle of big changes, and now you are heading for big changes yourself."

"Yes. Maybe we could talk a little about the year that has passed," I suggest. "Would you like to say more about the changes you have experienced?"

"It started of course with a breakup. It was difficult, but over time I succeeded in relating to Giulio in a new way."

Ask continues to summarise the year and the changes he has experienced.

"You can be quite spontaneous and expressive, Vikram. I like that. And now I can too."

I smile and nod. It's nice that he describes me in that way, directly, and that it is something positive, *spontaneous and expressive*.

"Speaking of which: I was really attracted to you when we first met," he continues. His cheeks redden. "I didn't say anything about it, but you guessed it perhaps. It was a little confusing, but it went just fine. I knew that nothing would happen between us. You're a great guy, Vikram. Antoine is lucky."

"Thanks, Ask. I also felt an attraction. So it was mutual. And I think that feeling desire and attraction in themselves has to be okay."

"Yes."

Maybe the final vestige of shame and guilt, including Giulio's accusations of being *pathological* and *puttano*, can be lifted. My vestige of shame also dissipates.

"And together with you, Ask, I have also gained a greater appreciation of holding back."

"That has meant a lot to me," he says. "You have given me validation that holding back can also be good. I can hold back, and I can express myself and be spontaneous."

"Now I just thought about your legs." We both laugh at the ambiguity. "I mean that you especially feel the power and the controlling in your legs. "That's good information that you can use in different situations."

"Yes. I'm more aware of holding back and that I can choose to continue with it or do something else now. And I can move between the poles, holding back and expressing myself in varying degrees."

It goes quiet a moment.

"Perhaps most importantly, Vikram, is that I haven't felt alone through all of these changes the last year. You have been there. That has meant a lot."

We look at one another. Swallow. I smile as some sort of reply. Then I inhale deeply. We need to talk more and directly about possibly ending therapy.

"I am glad that I have been able to follow you through these changes. We have shared much together. Yes, I have grown to like you, Ask. And now I wonder if this is heading towards an end. I don't know. You are welcome to continue with the therapy, but it is important that it's you who decides."

He might be afraid of ending therapy, I think. To end it with me. That I will die. Is he holding himself back? Am I holding him back?

"I'm also aware that it was now I who sent you the message. I suddenly feel a bit like Giulio. It's important that you don't continue out of consideration for me, feelings of guilt, fear, that it is difficult to finish with me or anything like that. If this is the case, let us explore it together. It could be beneficial. This is after all therapy that you pay for. It's your growth that's in focus here."

That hurts. *This is after all therapy that you pay for.* It physically hurts to say that. My chest and throat tighten. This is one of the paradoxes in therapy: it can be among our most intimate and beautiful experiences, but still it's a buy-and-sell relationship. Yet it is important to recall these boundaries, that in spite of everything we're not friends or ex-lovers, it is important to remind myself of this as well.

"Uh-huh," he says.

We continue talking for a while about endings, loss, and sorrow.

"In any case, this session is heading towards its end. It's still a little unclear for me whether this will be our last. I would like to thank you for our time together until now, Ask. And I will leave it up to you to contact me for a new session if and when you wish."

"Yes."

We stand up.

"Thanks for now, Vikram."

We go out into the foyer. He puts on his shoes. He turns towards me. Neither of us extends a hand.

"A hug?" he asks.
"Yes," I reply.
A quick hug.
"We'll be in touch, then," he says.
Will we?
"Yes," I say.
I close the door behind him.

I change into a shirt that I know Antoine likes. When he arrives, I am happy and kiss him. But he seems distant. We sit down on the sofa. He asks about the move, speaking somewhat indirectly and vaguely, that it must be hard for me, words like that. Yes, of course it is, but that doesn't mean that I won't do it. In the end I understand that he doesn't think that it's a good idea that I move now. In the end I understand that the changes between us have not been enough. In the end I understand that he has met somebody else. That's when I fall. That's how it feels. I'm sitting, but I imagine it, that feeling. It's as though I'm very small all of a sudden, an infant, and somebody has dropped me. And I fall. But I don't die, because I'm not an infant. I stand up and go into the therapy room.

I sit down in one chair. The other chair in front of me is empty. So it's over now? I lose my breath. In a way I expected this, but I am still in shock. I think: You are in shock, Vikram. Sense your feet on the floor. Sense the chair that supports your back and rear. You can also support yourself by asking for support. Isn't that what you often say to clients in a crisis? I call close friends and family. Set up a plan, pickups and drop offs as though I'm a little child. I need to be held by somebody, physically and metaphorically, now. I'm thankful that I have the courage to ask for support. I am thankful that the support exists. I also email my therapist and request a new session.

Once again I look at the empty chair in front of me. My God. I've finished with almost all of my clients. Should I contact them again and say that I'm staying after all? No, that can wait a little. And maybe I should wait with my therapy practice a few weeks anyway, until I have recovered somewhat. Yes, that is surely the best for both the clients and myself.

There's a little while before my first friend comes to pick me up. I look out through the window. There is the tree. I stand up, put on my shoes, and go outside. I sense the ground under my feet, and look up into green. I breathe.

Comments on "The empty chair"

Attraction in the therapy room: Both therapists and clients can experience attraction and infatuation in the therapy room. One study shows that 87 per cent of all therapists have experienced being attracted to clients at one point or another.[1] Many feel guilt and other discomfort even though they haven't broken any ethical rules or boundaries. Perhaps our early history when several therapists followed through on their attraction has contributed to making this topic especially taboo and shameful. Best known is probably the relationship between Carl Jung and Sabina Spielrein. In gestalt therapy we have Fritz Perls and Marty Fromm.

As a gestalt therapist I am concerned with holistic awareness. To feel desire or attraction is not wrong in itself. It is important to acknowledge attraction and to normalise it in order to avoid shame for both therapists and their clients. As long as attraction is shameful, there is a risk that therapists will not bring it up during supervision and closer examine the phenomenon.

Members of the Norwegian Gestalt Therapist Association (NGF) are obligated to follow the association's ethical guidelines that include the prohibition of abusing one's position sexually, and an encouragement to seek out therapy and supervision in the event of personal crises and when it is difficult to set limits for intimacy during therapy. The guidelines, information regarding complaints and much more is available on the association's website www.ngfo.no.

As a gestalt therapist I believe that whatever happens, happens here and now, is real and is a part of the relationship and the situation. When I as therapist experience attraction, it can provide information about something that is unfinished in me, something that I should examine more closely. At the same time, it can provide interesting information about the relationship and situation together with the client.

Parallel processes: This concept originates from psychoanalysis and ideas relating to transference and countertransference.[2] Parallel processes can imply that the therapist feels, thinks and acts towards a supervisor in a similar way as the client does in relation to the therapist, and the supervisor responds in a similar way as the therapist does with the client. Others understand the concept more broadly to include processes in the therapist's and client's relationships with parents, partners, and others.

As a gestalt therapist, however, I am concerned with there being something unique and real in every relationship and that the influence between individuals is mutual and not a simple linear cause-effect relationship. I don't use the terms transference and countertransference. Nevertheless, parallel processes can be a useful concept. I use it in the broad sense to imply similarities between processes in different relationships that are related to a therapy situation. Parallel processes are unavoidable. As always in gestalt therapy, our awareness is what's important.

In this story there are relationships between Ask on the one side and Bastian, Giulio and Nikolai on the other. In the therapy room there is a relationship between Ask and me that has some similarities to these. In my personal life I have a relationship with Antoine, which has similarities with Ask's romantic relationships and certain similarities with our therapeutic relationship. Partly this manifests in contact styles like retroflection and isolation from the one and expressiveness and confluence from the other. The projection of qualities like calm and expressiveness also play a role. Attraction, romantic relationships and endings are themes in several of the relationships.

As we see in the story, supervision can quickly become therapy when there are parallel processes. As a general rule, a therapist's supervisor and their own therapist should be two different people.

Suicide: During the last few years in Norway there have been 500 to 600 suicides per year.[3] Young men constitute the largest group. Risk factors include previous suicide attempts, depression, sexual abuse, bullying, social isolation, social-economic problems, unemployment, and access to information about suicide methods. Reactions among the surviving family and friends can vary significantly and can include shock and disbelief, loneliness, sadness, anger, reproach, guilt, and shame.

Love: Gestalt therapist Joseph Zinker associates falling in love with polarities and projection.[4] Often we fall in love via projections of blind spots in ourselves, poles that we are less aware of in ourselves but see in others. Over time this can lead to rigid roles and conflicts in the relationship. We can develop by integrating the entire polarity, by accepting and relating to ourselves and the other as whole persons. Love between people can arise in such "I-Thou" meetings.[5]

Attachment theory and contact styles: Attachment theory was first developed by the psychiatrist John Bowlby in the 50s and 60s.[6] Right from birth we seek closeness and safety from others. We smile, cry, and try all sorts of things. How we are met in these efforts contributes to which attachment styles we develop. Through experiments—especially the so-called "strange situation"—the psychologist Mary Ainsworth identified various attachment styles.[7] Some of us become anxious and emotionally expressive. Others hold more back and become avoidant. The styles can be triggered especially in situations where one feels the attachment is insecure, for example during conflicts. This is also becoming a dominant frame of reference for understanding how problems among adult romantic partners arise and can be addressed.[8]

Attachment theory resembles gestalt theories of contact and polarities. With attachment theory we get a further appreciation that the styles sit deeply within us right from infancy onwards. Some things often remain rather fixed. The avoidant and emotionally expressive styles in this story can maybe equate with the contact styles retroflection/isolation and expressiveness/confluence respectively. (Other important contact styles in the story include introjection with the message that Ask has killed Bastian and the demands and advice from Giulio and Nikolai, and projection that plays a role through both the attraction and alienation in various relationships).

Shaking and power in the legs: According to the trauma therapist Peter Levine, shaking can constitute an important part of the way one gets through trauma.[9] With Ask I encourage this after the difficult chair work with Giulio, and later he moves spontaneously after discovering the power in his legs. Maybe Ask's retroflection can also be related to the freeze reaction in the face of danger, and the unleashed power in his legs can be related to the fight or flight reactions.

Shock, support, and growth: While difficult incidents can have negative consequences such as post-traumatic stress, they can also lead to so-called post-traumatic growth.[10] Many begin to value certain relationships more and experience a new meaning to life. Seeking and receiving social support when one has experienced something painful and difficult can contribute to such growth.[11] More generally speaking, social support's crucial role in any growth has been highlighted by various gestalt therapists, including Laura Perls.[12]

NOTES

Chapter One

1. All citations and much of the information about Laura Perls is retrieved from Leibig, A. (Ed.) (1990). Laura Posner Perls—In memory. In: *Contact: A Newsletter and Networking Tool for the Gestalt Community*. Gouldsboro, ME: The Gestalt Journal. Available online at gestalt.org/laura.htm.
2. "There is no *I* taken in itself, but only the *I* of the primary word *I-Thou* and the *I* of the primary word *I-It*" Buber, M. (1937/2010). *I and Thou*. Eastford, CT: Martino Fine Books, p. 4.
3. Perls, F. (1942/1992). *Ego, Hunger and Aggression: A Revision of Freud's Theory and Method*. Gouldsboro, ME: The Gestalt Journal Press.
4. Perls, F., Hefferline, R., & Goodman, P. (1951/1994). *Gestalt Therapy: Excitement and Growth in the Human Personality*. Gouldsboro, ME: The Gestalt Journal Press.
5. See Barlow, A. R. (1981). Gestalt therapy and Gestalt psychology: Gestalt—antecedent influence or historical accident. *The Gestalt Journal*, IV(2). Available online at gestalt.org/barlow.htm.
6. James Simkin should be credited with this definition of gestalt therapy, according to Smith, E. W. L. (2003). *The Person of the Therapist*. Jefferson, NC: McFarland.

7. Perls, F., Hefferline, R., & Goodman, P. (1951/1994). *Gestalt Therapy: Excitement and Growth in the Human Personality*. Gouldsboro, ME: The Gestalt Journal Press.
8. Zeigarnik, B. (1927). Über das Behalten von erledigten und unerledigten Handlungen. *Psychologische Forschung, 9*.
9. Perls, F., Hefferline, R., & Goodman, P. (1951/1994). *Gestalt Therapy: Excitement and Growth in the Human Personality*. Gouldsboro, ME: The Gestalt Journal Press.
10. See for instance Perls, F. (1969). *Gestalt Therapy Verbatim*. Gouldsboro, ME: The Gestalt Journal Press.
11. The view of contact and contact styles has been changing. I build on the relational view presented in Wheeler, G. (1991). *Gestalt Reconsidered: A New Approach to Contact and Resistance*. Cleveland, OH: Gestalt Institute of Cleveland Press. This is also the view taken by the Norwegian Gestalt Institute, see for instance Jørstad, S. (2002). Oversikt over kontaktformer. In: A. Krüger & S. Jørstad (Ed.), *Den Flyvende Hollender*. Festskrift. Oslo: Norsk Gestaltinstitutt.
12. A metaphor means "understanding and experiencing one kind of thing in terms of another" (Lakoff, G., & Johnson, M. (2003/1980). *Metaphors We Live By*. Chicago, IL: The University of Chicago Press.) I associate this with projection. But maybe metaphors can also be generally understood as gestalts.
13. Perls, F. (1969). *Gestalt Therapy Verbatim*. Gouldsboro, ME: The Gestalt Journal Press. Fritz Perls, who was less relationally oriented in practice than many gestalt therapists today, uses the concept to describe inner conflicts. I believe that it can also apply to interpersonal conflicts.
14. See vol. II in Perls, F., Hefferline, R., & Goodman, P. (1951/1994). *Gestalt Therapy: Excitement and Growth in the Human Personality*. Gouldsboro, ME: The Gestalt Journal Press.
15. See among others: Stevens, J. O. (1971). *Awareness: Exploring, Experimenting, Experiencing*. Gouldsboro, ME: The Gestalt Journal Press; Zinker, J. (1977). *Creative Process in Gestalt Therapy*. New York: Random House; and Greenberg, L. S., & Kahn, S. E. (1978). Experimentation: A Gestalt approach to counselling. *Canadian Journal of Counselling and Psychotherapy, 13*(1).
16. For more about the history, applications and research, see Kellogg, S. H. (2015). *Transformational Chairwork: Using Psychotherapeutic Dialogues in Clinical Practice*. Lanham, MD: Rowman & Littlefield.
17. Ibid. It is important to remember that techniques do not make up the particular therapy. The therapeutic approach and the relationship are

crucial. In gestalt therapy, chair work should be used as an experiment, not to modify the client in the direction of a specific goal.
18. A relational approach—also using experiments—is emphasised more today than was previously the case. See in particular Wheeler, G. (1991). *Gestalt Reconsidered: A New Approach to Contact and Resistance*. Cleveland, OH: Gestalt Institute of Cleveland Press.

Chapter Two

1. Selye, H. (1936). A syndrome produced by diverse nocuous agents. *Nature*, 138. See also Selye, H. (1956). *The Stress of Life*. New York: McGraw-Hill.
2. Cohen, S., Janicki-Deverts, D., & Miller, G. E. (2007). Psychological stress and disease. *JAMA*, 298.
3. PubMed Health (2013). Depression: What is burnout syndrome? Available online at http://www.ncbi.nlm.nih.gov/pubmedhealth/.
4. Contrast with I-Thou relating. See Buber, M. (1937/2010). *I and Thou*. Eastford, CT: Martino Fine Books.
5. Beisser, A. (1970). Paradoxical theory of change. In: J. F Fagan & I. L Shepherd (Eds.), *Gestalt Therapy Now*. Gouldsboro, ME: The Gestalt Journal Press. Available online at gestalt.org/arnie.htm.
6. Mayo Clinic (2013). Stress relief from laughter? It's no joke. Available online at mayoclinic.org.
7. Skårderud, F. (2014). Den alvorlige leken. *Psykisk helse*, 2. Available online at psykiskhelse.no.
8. See also Jacobs, S. (2009). Humour in Gestalt therapy—Curative force and catalyst for change: A case study. *South African Journal of Psychology, 39*.
9. Bhikkhu Bodhi (2009). The Satipatthana Sutta. In: *The Middle Length Discourses of the Buddha*. Somerville, MA: Wisdom. Available online at wisdompubs.org.
10. For an updated version with references to several recent studies, see Kabat-Zinn, J. (2013). *Full Catastrophe Living (Revised and Updated Edition): Using the Wisdom of Your Body and Mind to Face Stress, Pain, and Illness*. New York: Bantam.
11. Roszak, T. (1996). The nature of sanity. *Psychology Today*, 1 January. Available online at psychologytoday.com.
12. See, for example, a recent study from Toronto, Canada, with references to other studies: Kardan, O. et al. (2015). Neighborhood greenspace and health in a large urban center. *Nature Scientific Reports, 5*. Available online at nature.com.

Chapter Three

1. Thuen, F., & Omland, T. (2008). Utroskap og psykisk helse: En undersøkelse av par som går i terapi. *Tidsskrift for Norsk Psykologforening,* 45(6). Available online at psykologtidsskriftet.no. p. 704.
2. Thuen, F., & Omland, T. (2008). Utroskap og psykisk helse: En undersøkelse av par som går i terapi. *Tidsskrift for Norsk Psykologforening,* 45(6). Available online at psykologtidsskriftet.no.
3. Ibid.
4. Posttraumatisk stresslidelse. *Helsebiblioteket.no.*
5. Malt, U. (2014). Posttraumatisk stresslidelse. *Store medisinske leksikon.* Available online at sml.snl.no.
6. Posttraumatisk stresslidelse. *Helsebiblioteket.no.*
7. Yehuda, R. et al. (1998). Phenomenology & psychobiology of the intergenerational response to trauma. In: Y. Danieli (Ed.), *International Handbook of Multigenerational Legacies of Trauma.* New York: Plenum. For a short introduction, see also Portney, C. (2003). Intergenerational transmission of trauma: An introduction for the clinician. *Psychiatric Times,* 1 April. Available online at psychiatrictimes.com.
8. Yehuda, R., & Bierer, L. M. (2009). The relevance of epigenetics to PTSD: Implications for the DSM-V. *Journal of Trauma Stress,* 22. See also Kellerman, N. P. F. (2013). Epigenetic transmission of holocaust trauma: Can nightmares be inherited? *Israel Journal of Psychiatry and Related Sciences,* 50(1).
9. See Sanford, N. (1966). *Self and Society: Social Change and Individual Development.* New York: Atherton.
10. Harris, E. S. (2007). Working with Forgiveness in Gestalt therapy. *Gestalt Review,* 11(2).
11. Ibid.
12. Duncan, B. L., Miller, S. D., Wampold, B. E., & Hubble, M. A. (Ed.) (2010). *The Heart and Soul of Change: Delivering What Works in Therapy.* Washington, DC: American Psychological Association.

Chapter Four

1. Thoresen, S., & Hjemdal, O. K. (Ed.) (2014). *Vold og voldtekt i Norge: En nasjonal forekomststudie av vold i et livsløpsperspektiv.* Oslo: Nasjonalt kunnskapssenter om vold og traumatisk stress. Available online at nkvts.no.

2. Ibid.
3. Stern, D. (2000). *The Interpersonal World of the Infant: A View from Psychoanalysis & Developmental Psychology*. New York: Basic.
4. Read more about sexual abuse, and working with confluence and counter-poles in Kolmannskog, V. (2014a). Voldtekt og konfluens: En kasusstudie av terapi med en overgrepsutsatt kvinne. *Norsk Gestalttidsskrift*, 11(2). Available online at Vikram.no.
5. Staemmler, F. M. (2012). *Empathy in Psychotherapy: How Therapists and Clients Understand Each Other*. New York: Springer.
6. Duncan, B. L., Miller, S. D., Wampold, B. E., & Hubble, M. A. (Ed.) (2010). *The Heart and Soul of Change: Delivering What Works in Therapy*. Washington, DC: American Psychological Association.
7. Putnam, F. W. (1989). Pierre Janet and modern views of dissociation. *Journal of Traumatic Stress*, 2(4).
8. Ibid.
9. Berlin, H. A., & Koch, C. (2009). Neuroscience meets psychoanalysis. *Scientific American Mind*, April/May. Available online at scientificamerican.com.
10. Ibid.
11. See Project Implicit at projectimplicit.net. Here you can take a test regarding your less conscious attitudes.
12. See Hooks, B. (2000). *Feminism is for Everybody: Passionate Politics*. Boston, MA: South EndPress.
13. Lakoff, G., & Johnson, M. (2003/1980). *Metaphors We Live By*. Chicago, IL: The University of Chicago Press.
14. Polster, E. (1987). *Every Person's Life is Worth a Novel*. Gouldsboro, ME: The Gestalt Journal Press.
15. One early example is Yalom, I., & Elkin, G. (1974). *Every Day Gets A Little Closer: A Twice-Told Therapy*. New York: Basic. A book that deals with sexual abuse is Axelsen, E. D., & Bakke, S. (1991). *Tilbakereisen: Om forandring gjennom terapi*. Oslo: Pax.
16. See, for example, Dossey, L. (1997). *Prayer is Good Medicine: How to Reap the Healing Benefits of Prayer*. New York: HarperOne.
17. For an overview of various gestalt approaches to dreams, see Jørstad, S. (2006). Å arbeide med drømmer i gestaltterapi. In: S. Jørstad & A. Krüger (Ed.), *Gestaltterapi i Praksis*. Oslo: Norsk Gestaltinstitutt.
18. See Freud, S. (1905/2006). *Fragment of an Analysis of Hysteria (Dora): Psychology of Love*. London: Penguin Classics.

19. Gilligan, C. (2011). *Joining the Resistance.* Cambridge: Polity. Also see Masson, J. (1985). *The Assault on Truth: Freud's Suppression of the Seduction Theory.* London: Penguin.
20. See for example Perls, F. (1969/1992). *Gestalt Therapy Verbatim.* Gouldsboro, ME: The Gestalt Journal Press.
21. Masson has criticised therapy in general based on such a view. See Masson, J. (1988). *Against Therapy: Emotional Tyranny and the Myth of Psychological Healing.* New York: Atheneum.
22. See among others: Hertenstein, M. J. et al. (2009). The communication of emotion via touch. *Emotion, 9*(4); and Field, T. et al. (2008). Massage therapy reduces pain in pregnant women, alleviates prenatal depression in both parents and improves their relationships. *Journal of Bodywork and Movement Therapies, 12*(2). For a concise overview of the positive effects of physical touch, also see Carey, B. (2010). Evidence that little touches do mean so much. *New York Times*, 22 February. Available online at nytimes.com.
23. Kringlen, E. (2002). Seksuelle overgrep, gjenvunnet hukommelse og multippel personlighetsforstyrrelse. *Tidsskrift for Den norske lægeforening*, 122. Available online at tidsskriftet.no.
24. See Loftus, E. F., & Palmer, J. C. (1974). Reconstruction of auto-mobile destruction: An example of the interaction between language and memory. *Journal of Verbal Learning and Verbal Behavior, 13*.
25. Milde, A. M. (2011). Narrativ eksponeringsterapi—en ny korttidsbehandling for komplekse og vedvarende traumatiske opplevelser. *Tidsskrift for Norsk Psykologforening, 48*(7). Available online at psykologtidsskriftet.no.
26. Also see Kolmannskog, V. (2014a). Voldtekt og konfluens: En kasusstudie av terapi med en overgrepsutsatt kvinne. *Norsk Gestalttidsskrift, 11*(2). Available online at Vikram.no.
27. Darwin, C. (1872). *The Expression of the Emotions in Man and Animals.* London: John Murray. Available online at darwin-online.org.uk.
28. Tomkins, S. S. (1963). *Affect Imagery Consciousness: Volume II, The Negative Affects.* New York: Springer.
29. Bradshaw, J. (1988). *Healing the Shame that Binds You.* Deerfield Beach, FL: Health Communications.
30. Also see Yontef, G. (1993). Shame. In: G. Yontef, *Awareness, Dialogue and Process: Essays on Gestalt Therapy.* Gouldsboro, ME: The Gestalt Journal Press. Also see Resnick, R. W. (1997). The "recursive loop" of shame: An alternative Gestalt therapy viewpoint. *Gestalt Review, 1*(3).

31. Wheeler, G. (1997). Self and shame: A Gestalt approach. *Gestalt Review, 1*(3).
32. Also see Yontef, G. (1993). Shame. In: G. Yontef, *Awareness, Dialogue and Process: Essays on Gestalt Therapy*. Gouldsboro, ME: The Gestalt Journal Press. Also see Wheeler, G. (1997). Self and shame: A Gestalt approach. *Gestalt Review, 1*(3).
33. See Valla, B. (2015). Hva pasientene har lært meg. *Psykologisk.no*, 30 January. Available online at psykologisk.no.
34. Duncan, B. L., Miller, S. D., Wampold, B. E., & Hubble, M. A. (Ed.) (2010). *The Heart and Soul of Change: Delivering What Works in Therapy*. Washington, DC: American Psychological Association.
35. Berge, T. (2005). Sekundærtraumatisering, vikarierende traumatisering og omsorgstretthet. *Tidsskrift for Norsk Psykologforening, 42*(2). Available online at www.psykologtidsskriftet.no.
36. Ibid.

Chapter Five

1. For a short summary of prison research and an introduction to sociology of law, see Mathiesen, T. (2011). *Retten i samfunnet: En innføring i rettssosiologi*. Oslo: Pax.
2. Smith, P. S., Horn, T., Nilsen, J. F., & Rua, M. (2013). Isolasjon i skandinaviske fengsler: Skandinavisk praksis og etableringen av et skandinavisk isolasjonsnettverk. *Kritisk Juss, 39*. Available online at jus.uio.no.
3. Ibid.
4. For a short overview and criticism, see Sloan, R. P. (2011). A fighting spirit won't save your life. *New York Times*, 24 January. Available online at nytimes.com.
5. Buber, M. (1937/2010). *I and Thou*. Eastford, CT: Martino Fine Books.
6. Ekenstam, C. (1998). En historia om manlig gråt. In: C. Ekenstam et al. (Ed.), *Rädd att falla: studier i manlighet*. Örlinge: Gidlunds förlag. See a summary and interview with Ekenstam in Sandnes, H. E. (2010). Store gutter gråter ikke. *Kilden*, 7 September. Available online at kilden.forskningsradet.no.

Chapter Six

1. Roland, E., & Gauestad, E. (2009). *Seksuell orientering og mobbing*. Stavanger: University of Stavanger. Available online at udir.no

2. Sue, D. W. (2010). Microaggressions: More than just race. *Psychology Today*, 17 November. Available online at psychologytoday.com.
3. Goodman, P. (1977). The politics of being queer. In: T. Stoehr (Ed.), *Nature Heals: The Psychological Essays of Paul Goodman*. Gouldsboro, ME: The Gestalt Journal Press.
4. Perls, F., Hefferline, R., & Goodman, P. (1951/1994). *Gestalt Therapy: Excitement and Growth in the Human Personality*. Gouldsboro, ME: The Gestalt Journal Press.
5. Cooley, C. H. (1902). *Human Nature and the Social Order*. New York: C. Scribner's sons. For more information about the self and self-image according to symbolic interactionism and other socially oriented theories, also see Hogg, M. A., & Vaughan, G. M. (2011). *Social Psychology*. Essex: Pearson Education.
6. Lasch, C. (1979). *The Culture of Narcissism: American Life in an Age of Diminishing Expectations*. New York: W. W. Norton.
7. Yontef, G. (1993). Treating people with character disorders. In: G. Yontef, *Awareness, Dialogue and Process: Essays on Gestalt Therapy*. Gouldsboro, ME: The Gestalt Journal Press.
8. Buber, M. (1937/2010). *I and Thou*. Eastford, CT: Martino Fine Books.
9. See for example Burgo, J. (2013). All bullies are narcissists. *The Atlantic*, 14 November. Available online at theatlantic.com.
10. Zinker, J. (1977). *Creative Process in Gestalt Therapy*. New York: Random House.
11. Seligman, M. (2004). *Authentic Happiness: Using the New Positive Psychology to Realize Your Potential for Lasting Fulfillment*. New York: Atria. Also see the TED-talk Seligman, M. (2004). The new era of positive psychology. *TED*. Available online at ted.com.
12. "… if you are selfish, you should be wisely selfish. Ordinary selfishness focuses only on your own needs, but if you are wisely selfish, you will treat others just as well as you treat those close to you. Ultimately, this strategy will produce more satisfaction, more happiness." Dalai Lama & Hopkins, J. (2002). *How to Practice: The Way to a Meaningful Life*. New York: Atria, p. 81.
13. For an English translation and version, see Amaravati Sangha (2013). Karaniya metta sutta: The Buddha's words on loving-kindness (Sn 1.8). *Access to Insight (Legacy Edition)*, 2 November. Available online at accesstoinsight.org.
14. Salzberg, S. (1995). *Lovingkindness: The Revolutionary Art of Happiness*. Boulder, CO: Shambhala.

15. Fredrickson, B. L., Cohn, M. A., Coffey, K. A., Pek, J., & Finkel, S. M. (2008). Open hearts build lives: Positive emotions, induced through loving-kindness meditation, build consequential personal resources. *Journal of Personality and Social Psychology, 95*(5). Also see Fredrickson, B. L. (2013). *Love 2.0: Finding Happiness and Health in Moments of Connection*. New York: Plume.
16. Kellogg, S. H. (2015). *Transformational Chairwork: Using Psychotherapeutic Dialogues in Clinical Practice*. Lanham, MD: Rowman & Littlefield.
17. Neff, K. (2011). *Self-compassion*. New York: HarperCollins. Also see the TED talk Neff, K. (2013). The space between self-esteem and self-compassion. *TED*. Available online at ted.com.
18. Ibid.

Chapter Seven

1. See also Levine, P. (1997). *Wakening the Tiger: Healing Trauma*. Berkeley, CA: North Atlantic.
2. Ibid.
3. Kepner, J. (1993/2013). *Body Process: A Gestalt Approach to Working with the Body in Psychotherapy*. New York: Routledge.
4. Eberhard-Gran, M., Schei, B., & Eskild, A. (2007). Somatic symptoms and diseases are more common in women exposed to violence. *Journal of General Internal Medicine, 22*(12).
5. Also see Øverenget, E. (2015). Kunsten å ikke vise seg frem. *Verdens Gang*, 29 March. Available online at vg.no.
6. Levitsky, A., & Perls, F. (1969). The rules and games of gestalt therapy. In: H. M Ruitenbeek (Ed.), *Group Therapy Today: Styles, Methods and Techniques*. New York: Atherton.

Chapter Eight

1. Van der Ros, J. (2013). Alskens folk: Levekår, livssituasjon og livskvalitet for personer med kjønnsidentitetstematikk. Likestillingssenteret. Available online at bufdir.no.
2. Helsedirektoratet (2015). Rett til rett kjønn—helse til alle kjønn: Utredning av vilkår for endring av juridisk kjønn og organisering av helsetjenester for personer som opplever kjønnsinkongruens og kjønnsdysfori. Available online at regjeringen.no.

3. See Regjeringen (2015). Høring—forslag til lov om endring av juridisk kjønn, 25 June. Available online at regjeringen.no. Also see Espseth, L. D. (2015). Kjønnet mitt er ute på høring. *Dagbladet*, 26 June. Available online at dagbladet.no.
4. Kolmannskog, V. (2014b). Gestalt approaches to gender identity issues: A case study of a transgender therapy group in Oslo. *Gestalt Review, 18*(3). Also see Kolmannskog, V. (2013). Kjønnsidentitet og polaritetsteori: En kasusstudie av en samtalegruppe med transpersoner. *Norsk Gestalttidsskrift, 10*(2). Both are available online at Vikram.no.
5. Yalom, I. (2005). *Theory and Practice of Group Psychotherapy* (5th edn). New York: Basic.
6. See several relevant chapters in Jacobs, L., & Hycner, R. (Eds.) (2010). *Relational Approaches in Gestalt Therapy*. New York: Routledge. Also see Feder, B., & Frew, J. (Eds.) (2008). *Beyond the Hot Seat Revisited: Gestalt Approaches to Group*. New York: Brunner/Mazel.
7. See for instance Lodahl, M. A. (2013). Ending the straight world order. *TEDxCopenhagen*. Available online at tedxtalks.ted.com.

Chapter Nine

1. Pope, K. S., Tabachnik, B. G., & Keith-Spiege, P. (1986). Sexual attraction of clients: The human therapist and the (sometimes) inhuman training system. *American Psychologist, 41*(2). Available online at kspope.com.
2. The concept was first used by Searles, H. F. (1955). The informational value of the supervisor's emotional experience. *Psychiatry, 18*. For an overview of the psychoanalytic concept, see also Sumerel, M. B. (1994). Parallel process in supervision. *ERIC Digest, 4*. Available online at ericdigests.org.
3. Information is retrieved from the website to the National Center for Suicide Research and Prevention: med.uio.no/klinmed/forskning/sentre/nssf. Last retrieved 1 July 2015.
4. Zinker, J. (1977). *Creative Process in Gestalt Therapy*. New York: Random House.
5. Buber, M. (1937/2010). *I and Thou*. Eastford, CT: Martino Fine Books.
6. For a new and updated edition, see Bowlby, J. (1983). *Attachment and Loss: Volume I*. New York: Basic. The trilogy *Attachment and Loss* was first published between 1969 and 1980.

7. Ainsworth, M. D. S., & Bell, S. M. (1970). Attachment, exploration, and separation: Illustrated by the behaviour of one-year-olds in a strange situation. *Child Development, 41*(1).
8. See Gran, S. (2008). *Kjærlighetens tre porter*. Oslo: Aschehoug.
9. Levine, P. (1997). *Wakening the Tiger: Healing Trauma*. Berkeley, CA: North Atlantic.
10. Tedeschi, R. G., & Calhoun, L. (2004). Posttraumatic growth: A new perspective on psychotraumatology. *Psychiatric Times*, 1 April. Available online at psychiatrictimes.com.
11. See Yu, Y., et al. (2014). Resilience and social support promote posttraumatic growth of women with infertility: The mediating role of positive coping. *Psychiatry Research, 215*(2).
12. Perls, L. (1969). *Living at the Boundary*. Gouldsboro, ME: The Gestalt Journal Press. Also see Leibig, A. (Ed.) (1990). Laura Posner Perls—In memory. *Contact: A Newsletter and Networking Tool for the Gestalt Community*. Gouldsboro, ME: The Gestalt Journal. Available online at gestalt.org/laura.htm.

REFERENCES

Ainsworth, M. D. S., & Bell, S. M. (1970). Attachment, exploration, and separation: Illustrated by the behaviour of one-year-olds in a strange situation. *Child Development, 41*(1).
Amaravati, S. (2013). Karaniya metta sutta: The Buddha's words on loving-kindness (Sn 1.8). *Access to Insight (Legacy Edition)*, 2 November. Available online at accesstoinsight.org.
Axelsen, E. D., & Bakke, S. (1991). *Tilbakereisen: Om forandring gjennom terapi.* Oslo: Pax.
Barlow, A. R. (1981). Gestalt therapy and Gestalt psychology: Gestalt—antecedent influence or historical accident. *The Gestalt Journal, IV*(2). Available online at gestalt.org/barlow.htm.
Beisser, A. (1970). Paradoxical theory of change. In: J. F Fagan & I. L Shepherd (Eds.), *Gestalt Therapy Now*. Gouldsboro, ME: The Gestalt Journal Press. Available online at gestalt.org/arnie.htm.
Berge, T. (2005). Sekundærtraumatisering, vikarierende traumatisering og omsorgstretthet. *Tidsskrift for Norsk Psykologforening, 42*(2). Available online at www.psykologtidsskriftet.no.
Berlin, H. A., & Koch, C. (2009). Neuroscience meets psychoanalysis. *Scientific American Mind*, April/May. Available online at scientificamerican.com.
Bhikkhu, B. (2009). The Satipatthana Sutta. In: *The Middle Length Discourses of the Buddha*. Somerville, MA: Wisdom. Available online at wisdompubs.org.

Björk, N. (2007). Söndagskolumnen. *Dagens Nyheter*, 25 March. Available online in Swedish at dn.se.

Bowlby, J. (1983). *Attachment and Loss: Volume I*. New York: Basic.

Bradshaw, J. (1988). *Healing the Shame that Binds You*. Deerfield Beach, FL: Health Communications.

Buber, M. (1937). *I and Thou*. Eastford, CT: Martino Fine Books [reprinted 2010].

Burgo, J. (2013). All bullies are narcissists. *The Atlantic*, 14 November. Available online at theatlantic.com.

Carey, B. (2010). Evidence that little touches do mean so much. *New York Times*, 22 February. Available online at nytimes.com.

Cohen, S., Janicki-Deverts, D., & Miller, G. E. (2007). Psychological stress and disease. *JAMA*, 298.

Cooley, C. H. (1902). *Human Nature and the Social Order*. New York: C. Scribner's sons.

Dalai Lama, & Hopkins, J. (2002). *How to Practice: The Way to a Meaningful Life*. New York: Atria.

Darwin, C. (1872). *The Expression of the Emotions in Man and Animals*. London: John Murray. Available online at darwin-online.org.uk.

Dossey, L. (1997). *Prayer is Good Medicine: How to Reap the Healing Benefits of Prayer*. New York: HarperOne.

Duncan, B. L., Miller, S. D., Wampold, B. E., & Hubble, M. A. (Ed.) (2010). *The Heart and Soul of Change: Delivering What Works in Therapy*. Washington, DC: American Psychological Association.

Eberhard-Gran, M., Schei, B., & Eskild, A. (2007). Somatic symptoms and diseases are more common in women exposed to violence. *Journal of General Internal Medicine*, 22(12).

Ekenstam, C. (1998). En historia om manlig gråt. In: C. Ekenstam et al. (Ed.), *Rädd att falla: studier i manlighet*. Örlinge: Gidlunds förlag.

Espseth, L. D. (2015). Kjønnet mitt er ute på høring. *Dagbladet*, 26 June. Available online at dagbladet.no.

Feder, B., & Frew, J. (Eds.) (2008). *Beyond the Hot Seat Revisited: Gestalt Approaches to Group*. New York: Brunner/Mazel.

Field, T., et al. (2008). Massage therapy reduces pain in pregnant women, alleviates prenatal depression in both parents and improves their relationships. *Journal of Bodywork and Movement Therapies*, 12(2).

Fredrickson, B. L. (2013). *Love 2.0: Finding Happiness and Health in Moments of Connection*. New York: Plume.

Fredrickson, B. L., Cohn, M. A., Coffey, K. A., Pek, J., & Finkel, S. M. (2008). Open Hearts Build Lives: Positive Emotions, Induced Through Loving-Kindness Meditation, Build Consequential Personal Resources. *Journal of Personality and Social Psychology*, 95(5).

Freud, S. (1905). *Fragment of an Analysis of Hysteria (Dora): Psychology of Love*. London: Penguin Classics [reprinted 2006].
Gilligan, C. (2011). *Joining the Resistance*. Cambridge: Polity.
Goodman, P. (1977). The politics of being queer. In: T. Stoehr (Ed.), *Nature Heals: The Psychological Essays of Paul Goodman*. Gouldsboro, ME: The Gestalt Journal Press.
Gran, S. (2008). *Kjærlighetens tre porter*. Oslo: Aschehoug.
Gran, S. (2014). Diagnose: Overveldelse. *Morgenbladet*, 25 September. Available online at morgenbladet.no.
Greenberg, L. S., & Kahn, S. E. (1978). Experimentation: A Gestalt approach to counselling. *Canadian Journal of Counselling and Psychotherapy*, 13(1).
Hahn, T. N. (1999). *The Miracle of Mindfulness*. Boston, MA: Beacon Press.
Hanh, T. N. (2008). The moment is perfect. *Shambhala Sun*, May 2008. Available online at lionsroar.com.
Harris, E. S. (2007). Working with forgiveness in Gestalt therapy. *Gestalt Review*, 11(2).
Helsebiblioteket.no Posttraumatisk stresslidelse.
Helsedirektoratet (2015). Rett til rett kjønn—helse til alle kjønn: Utredning av vilkår for endring av juridisk kjønn og organisering av helsetjenester for personer som opplever kjønnsinkongruens og kjønnsdysfori. Available online at regjeringen.no.
Hertenstein, M. J., et al. (2009). The communication of emotion via touch. *Emotion*, 9(4).
Hogg, M. A., & Vaughan, G. M. (2011). *Social Psychology*. Essex: Pearson Education.
Hooks, B. (2000). *Feminism is for Everybody: Passionate Politics*. Boston, MA: South End Press.
Jacobs, L., & Hycner, R. (Eds.) (2010). *Relational Approaches in Gestalt Therapy*. New York: Routledge.
Jacobs, S. (2009). Humour in Gestalt therapy—Curative force and catalyst for change: A case study. *South African Journal of Psychology*, 39.
Jørstad, S. (2002). Oversikt over kontaktformer. In: A. Krüger & S. Jørstad (Ed.), *Den Flyvende Hollender*. Festskrift. Oslo: Norsk Gestaltinstitutt.
Jørstad, S. (2006). Å arbeide med drømmer i gestaltterapi. In: A. Jørstad & S. Krüger (Ed.), *Gestaltterapi i Praksis*. Oslo: Norsk Gestaltinstitutt.
Kabat-Zinn, J. (2013). *Full Catastrophe Living (Revised and Updated Edition): Using the Wisdom of Your Body and Mind to Face Stress, Pain, and Illness*. New York: Bantam.
Kardan, O., et al. (2015). Neighborhood greenspace and health in a large urban center. *Nature Scientific Reports*, 5.

Kellerman, N. P. F. (2013). Epigenetic transmission of holocaust trauma: Can nightmares be inherited? *Israel Journal of Psychiatry and Related Sciences*, 50(1).

Kellogg, S. H. (2015). *Transformational Chairwork: Using Psychotherapeutic Dialogues in Clinical Practice*. Lanham, MD: Rowman & Littlefield.

Kepner, J. (1993). *Body Process: A Gestalt Approach to Working with the Body in Psychotherapy*. New York: Routledge [reprinted 2013].

Kolmannskog, V. (2013). Kjønnsidentitet og polaritetsteori: En kasusstudie av en samtalegruppe med transpersoner. *Norsk Gestalttidsskrift*, 10(2).

Kolmannskog, V. (2014a). Voldtekt og konfluens: En kasusstudie av terapi med en overgrepsutsatt kvinne. *Norsk Gestalttidsskrift*, 11(2). Available online at Vikram.no

Kolmannskog, V. (2014b). Gestalt approaches to gender identity issues: A case study of a transgender therapy group in Oslo. *Gestalt Review*, 18(3).

Kringlen, E. (2002). Seksuelle overgrep, gjenvunnet hukommelse og multippel personlighetsforstyrrelse. *Tidsskrift for Den norske lægeforening*, 122. Available online at tidsskriftet.no.

Lakoff, G., & Johnson, M. (1980). *Metaphors We Live By*. Chicago, IL: The University of Chicago Press [reprinted 2003].

Lasch, C. (1979). *The Culture of Narcissism: American Life in an Age of Diminishing Expectations*. New York: W. W. Norton.

Leibig, A. (Ed.) (1990). Laura Posner Perls—In memory. *Contact: A Newsletter and Networking Tool for the Gestalt Community*. Gouldsboro, ME: The Gestalt Journal. Available online at gestalt.org/laura.htm.

Levine, P. (1997). *Wakening the Tiger: Healing Trauma*. Berkeley, CA: North Atlantic.

Levitsky, A., & Perls, F. (1969). The rules and games of Gestalt therapy. In: H. M. Ruitenbeek (Ed.), *Group Therapy Today: Styles, Methods and Techniques*. New York: Atherton.

Lodahl, M. A. (2013). Ending the straight world order. *TEDxCopenhagen*. Available online at tedxtalks.ted.com.

Loftus, E. F., & Palmer, J. C. (1974). Reconstruction of auto-mobile destruction: An example of the interaction between language and memory. *Journal of Verbal Learning and Verbal Behavior*, 13.

Malkin, J. (2003). *Lion's Roar*, 1 July. Available online at lionsroar.com.

Malt, U. (2014). Posttraumatisk stresslidelse. *Store medisinske leksikon*. Available online at sml.snl.no.

Masson, J. (1985). *The Assault on Truth: Freud's Suppression of the Seduction Theory*. London: Penguin.

Masson, J. (1988). *Against Therapy: Emotional Tyranny and the Myth of Psychological Healing*. New York: Atheneum.

Mathiesen, T. (2011). *Retten i samfunnet: En innføring i rettssosiologi*. Oslo: Pax.
Mayo Clinic. (2013). Stress relief from laughter? It's no joke. Available online at mayoclinic.org.
Milde, A. M. (2011). Narrativ eksponeringsterapi—en ny korttidsbehandling for komplekse og vedvarende traumatiske opplevelser. *Tidsskrift for Norsk Psykologforening, 48*(7). Available online at psykologtidsskriftet.no.
National Center for Suicide Research and Prevention: med.uio.no/klinmed/ forskning/sentre/nssf.
Neff, K. (2011). *Self-compassion*. New York: HarperCollins.
Neff, K. (2013). The space between self-esteem and self-compassion. *TED*. Available online at ted.com.
Øverenget, E. (2015). Kunsten å ikke vise seg frem. *Verdens Gang*, 29 March. Available online at vg.no.
Perls, F. (1942). *Ego, Hunger and Aggression: A Revision of Freud's Theory and Method*. Gouldsboro, ME: The Gestalt Journal Press [reprinted 1992].
Perls, F. (1969). *Gestalt Therapy Verbatim*. Gouldsboro, ME: The Gestalt Journal Press.
Perls, F., Hefferline, R., & Goodman, P. (1951). *Gestalt Therapy: Excitement and Growth in the Human Personality*. Gouldsboro, ME: The Gestalt Journal Press [reprinted 1994].
Perls, L. (1969). *Living at the Boundary*. Gouldsboro, ME: The Gestalt Journal Press.
Polster, E. (1987). *Every Person's Life is Worth a Novel*. Gouldsboro, ME: The Gestalt Journal Press.
Pope, K. S., Tabachnik, B. G., & Keith-Spiege, P. (1986). Sexual attraction of clients: The human therapist and the (sometimes) inhuman training system. *American Psychologist, 41*(2). Available online at kspope.com.
Portney, C. (2003). Intergenerational transmission of trauma: An introduction for the clinician. *Psychiatric Times*, 1 April. Available online at psychiatrictimes.com.
PubMed Health. (2013). Depression: What is burnout syndrome? Available online at http://www.ncbi.nlm.nih.gov/pubmedhealth/.
Purser, R., & Loy, D. (2013). Beyond McMindfulness. *Huffington Post*, 1 July. Available online at huffingtonpost.com.
Putnam, F. W. (1989). Pierre Janet and modern views of dissociation. *Journal of Traumatic Stress, 2*(4).
Regjeringen (2015). Høring—forslag til lov om endring av juridisk kjønn. 25 June. Available online at regjeringen.no.
Resnick, R. W. (1997). The "recursive loop" of shame: An alternative Gestalt therapy viewpoint. *Gestalt Review, 1*(3).

Roland, E., & Gauestad, E. (2009). *Seksuell orientering og mobbing.* Stavanger: University of Stavanger. Available online at udir.no.
Roszak, T. (1996). The nature of sanity. *Psychology Today*, 1 January. Available online at psychologytoday.com.
Salzberg, S. (1995). *Lovingkindness: The Revolutionary Art of Happiness.* Boulder, CO: Shambhala.
Sandnes, H. E. (2010). Store gutter gråter ikke. *Kilden*, 7 September. Available online at kilden.forskningsradet.no.
Sanford, N. (1966). *Self and Society: Social Change and Individual Development.* New York: Atherton.
Searles, H. F. (1955). The informational value of the supervisor's emotional experience. *Psychiatry, 18.*
Seligman, M. (2004). *Authentic Happiness: Using the New Positive Psychology to Realize Your Potential for Lasting Fulfillment.* New York: Atria.
Selye, H. (1936). A syndrome produced by diverse nocuous agents. *Nature, 138.*
Selye, H. (1956). *The Stress of Life.* New York: McGraw-Hill.
Skårderud, F. (2014). Den alvorlige leken. *Psykisk helse, 2.* Available online at psykiskhelse.no.
Sloan, R. P. (2011). A fighting spirit won't save your life. *New York Times*, 24 January. Available online at nytimes.com.
Smith, E. W. L. (2003). *The Person of the Therapist.* Jefferson, NC: McFarland.
Smith, P. S., Horn, T., Nilsen, J. F., & Rua, M. (2013). Isolasjon i skandinaviske fengsler. Skandinavisk praksis og etableringen av et skandinavisk isolasjonsnettverk. *Kritisk Juss, 39.* Available online at jus.uio.no.
Staemmler, F. M. (2012). *Empathy in Psychotherapy: How Therapists and Clients Understand Each Other.* New York: Springer.
Stern, D. (2000). *The Interpersonal World of the Infant: A View from Psychoanalysis & Developmental Psychology.* New York: Basic.
Stevens, J. O. (1971). *Awareness: Exploring, Experimenting, Experiencing.* Gouldsboro, ME: The Gestalt Journal Press.
Sue, D. W. (2010). Microaggressions: More than just race. *Psychology Today*, 17 November. Available online at psychologytoday.com.
Sumerel, M. B. (1994). Parallel process in supervision. *ERIC Digest, 4.* Available online at ericdigests.org.
Tedeschi, R. G., & Calhoun, L. (2004). Posttraumatic growth: A new perspective on psychotraumatology. *Psychiatric Times*, 1 April. Available online at psychiatrictimes.com.
Thoresen, S., & Hjemdal, O. K. (Ed.) (2014). *Vold og voldtekt i Norge: En nasjonal forekomststudie av vold i et livsløpsperspektiv.* Oslo: Nasjonalt kunnskapssenter om vold og traumatisk stress. Available online at nkvts.no.

Thuen, F., & Omland, T. (2008). Utroskap og psykisk helse: En undersøkelse av par som går i terapi. *Tidsskrift for Norsk Psykologforening*, 45(6). Available online at psykologtidsskriftet.no.
Tomkins, S. S. (1963). *Affect Imagery Consciousness: Volume II, The Negative Affects*. New York: Springer.
Valla, B. (2015). Hva pasientene har lært meg. *Psykologisk.no*, 30 January. Available online at psykologisk.no.
Van der Ros, J. (2013). Alskens folk: Levekår, livssituasjon og livskvalitet for personer med kjønnsidentitetstematikk. Likestillingssenteret. Available online at bufdir.no.
Wedge, M. (2013). After the infidelity: Can counseling help? *Psychology Today*, 18 September. Available online at psychologytoday.com.
Wheeler, G. (1991). *Gestalt Reconsidered: A New Approach to Contact and Resistance*. Cleveland, OH: Gestalt Institute of Cleveland Press.
Wheeler, G. (1997). Self and shame: A Gestalt approach. *Gestalt Review*, 1(3).
Yalom, I. (2005). *Theory and Practice of Group Psychotherapy* (5th edn). New York: Basic.
Yalom, I., & Elkin, G. (1974). *Every Day Gets A Little Closer: A Twice-Told Therapy*. New York: Basic.
Yehuda, R., & Bierer, L. M. (2009). The relevance of epigenetics to PTSD: Implications for the DSM-V. *Journal of Trauma Stress*, 22.
Yehuda, R., et al. (1998). Phenomenology & psychobiology of the intergenerational response to trauma. In: Y. Danieli (Ed.), *International Handbook of Multigenerational Legacies of Trauma*. New York: Plenum.
Yontef, G. (1993). *Awareness, Dialogue and Process: Essays on Gestalt Therapy*. Gouldsboro, ME: The Gestalt Journal Press.
Yu, Y., et al. (2014). Resilience and social support promote posttraumatic growth of women with infertility: The mediating role of positive coping. *Psychiatry Research*, 215(2).
Zeigarnik, B. (1927). Über das Behalten von erledigten und unerledigten Handlungen. *Psychologische Forschung*, 9.
Zinker, J. (1977). *Creative Process in Gestalt Therapy*. New York: Random House.

INDEX

abuse and sexual fantasies, 49–50, 64–65
Affect Imagery Consciousness, 156
Ainsworth, M. D. S., 161
alone, experience of being, 44, 61
Amaravati, S., 158
"around the world" phenomenon, 94–95
attachment theory, 149–150
attraction in therapy room, 148
"awareness", 6
    becoming whole as societies, 12
    holistic, 82–83
    strengthening client's, 7
    of sensitivity, 88
Axelsen, E. D., 155

Bakke, S., 155
Barlow, A. R., 151
becoming whole as societies, 12
Beisser, A., 9, 153
Bell, S. M., 161

Berge, T., 157
Berlin, H. A., 155
betrayal, 29
    chair work, 31–32, 35–36
    control and responsibility, 34
    counter-poles to control, 33–34
    effectiveness of therapy, 41
    forgiveness, 35, 37, 41
    guided fantasy, 39
    hamster wheel experiment, 32–33
    here and now, 37–38
    holding back feelings, 31
    infidelity, 34, 40
    post-traumatic stress, 40
    relational meditation, 38
    support and challenge, 41
    suspicion after experiencing infidelity, 30
    transformational experiences, 37
    transmission of trauma, 29
Bhikkhu, B., 153
Bierer, L. M., 154

Björk, N., 25
blanket experiment to avoid physical contact, 107–109
blind spots, 12
Bowlby, J., 149, 160
Bradshaw, J., 156
Buber, M., 3, 8, 27, 151, 153, 157, 158, 160
Burgo, J., 158
burnout, 19, 25
  activities after, 22–23
  syndrome, 153

Calhoun, L., 161
Carey, B., 156
chair work, 14, 75–77 *see also*: guided fantasy; here and now
  betrayal, 31–32, 35–36
  to explore relationship, 133–134, 140
  in holding back, 97–99
  in self first, 85–86
  two-chair work, 14
change as paradoxical process, 9
client and therapist relationship, 14
  see also: empty chair
Coffey, K. A., 159
Cohen, S., 25, 153
Cohn, M. A., 159
communication through reflections, 56
"confluence", 11, 61–62
connecting to breathing, 20
contact as first reality, 9
  blind spots, 12
  "confluence", 11
  "contact styles", 9–10, 11
  "deflection", 11
  inherent factors in person's life, 9
  internalised oppression, 10
  interpretations of therapist and client, 10
  introjection, 10
  metaphors to understand world, 10
  polarity, 11–12
  projection, 10
  "retroflection", 10–11

contact styles, 9–10, 11, 150, 152
control and responsibility, 34
Cooley, C. H., 158
counter-poles, 33–34, 135

Dalai Lama, 158
Darwin, C., 156
death perspective on life, 23
"deflection", 11
demands exceeding adaptive capacity, 25
dialogical approach, 6
dialogical relationships, 4, 9
dissociation, 45, 51, 62–63
distancing from all, 101
Dossey, L., 155
dream exploration, 64
Duncan, B. L., 154, 155, 157

Eberhard-Gran, M., 159
ecopsychology, 27
Ekenstam, C., 157
Elkin, G., 155
emotion communication via touch, 156
empty chair, 14, 129, 147
  attachment theory, 149–150
  attraction in therapy room, 148
  build up of frustration, 141
  chair work, 133–134, 140
  contact styles, 150
  counter-pole, 135
  end of supervision relationship, 139–140
  expressive nature, 145
  giving space to feelings, 139
  guided fantasy, 136–137
  guilt and shame, 135
  here and now, 142–143
  holding back, 131, 135, 136, 145–146
  love, 149
  metaphor for war, 138
  metta, 140–141
  outcome, 139
  painful polarization, 140
  paradox in therapy, 146
  parallel processes, 148–149

patient's state of mind when
    understood, 132
post-traumatic growth, 150
power in legs, 150
problems in relationship, 143, 144
shaking, 150
social support, 150
suicide, 149
therapist's love, 138, 145, 146, 147, 148
uncertainty and need for control in
    relationship, 130
understanding the patient, 131
Eskild, A., 159
Espseth, L. D., 160
Excitement and Growth in the Human
    Personality, 5
exhale to calm nervous system, 44
existentialism, 25–26
"experiment", 13–15 *see also*:
    "awareness"; guided fantasy;
    here and now; metta
    "chair work", 14
    client and therapist relationship, 14
    empty chair, the, 14
    guided awareness, 13
    role of language, 13
    two-chair work, 14
exploring two poles, 107
Expression of the Emotions in Man
    and Animals, 156
expressive nature, 145

false memories, 49
Feder, B., 160
feedback from clients, 66
feeling the foundation, 43
Feldenkrais and Alexander methods, 3
Field, T., 156
figure-ground perception, 11
Finkel, S. M., 159
flowing together, 58, 61–62
forgiveness, 35, 37, 41
Frankfurt University, lecture at, 1
Fredrickson, B. L., 159
freeze, 97, 110
    abuse and cancer, 110–111

afraid and explode, 100–101
angry side, 101, 106
blanket experiment to avoid
    physical contact, 107–109
body work and boundaries, 110
chair work, 97–99
distancing from all, 101
exploring two poles, 107
knowing better of oneself, 101
perceived as uncomfortable, 99
projected counter-pole, 102
putting words on something
    wordless, 103–105
secrets and secrecy, 111
therapy with abused clients, 110
Freud, S., 49, 155
Frew, J., 160
Friedrich, 2, 3 *see also*: Goodman, P.;
    Posner, L.
    art and literature, 4
    book, 4
    death, 5
    rupture with orthodox
        psychoanalysts, 4
    tension between Laura and, 5
frustration, build up of, 141

Gauestad, E., 157
Gelb, A., 1
gender identity, 126
gender-neutral toilets, 116
gender norms, 127
gestalt, 2
    approaches to dreams, 155
    figure-ground perception, 11
    institute, 5
    psychology, 1
    fixed, 8
gestalt therapist, 144
    as psychoanalysts, 49–50
gestalt therapy, 2–3, 70, 151, 156 *see also*:
    here and now; I and Thou
    "awareness", 6, 7
    body-oriented, 6–7
    change as paradoxical process, 9
    dialogical approach, 6

Excitement and Growth in the
    Human Personality, 5
"experiment", 13–15
here and now, 2, 3, 6, 7, 9
holistic awareness, 82
humour in, 153
I and Thou, 6
inner dialogue, 7
metta, 89–90
mindfulness and sensing here
    and now, 46
person as part of situation, 9
professionalism linked to
    awareness, 9
relating to each other here and
    now, 71
strengthening client's awareness, 7
for transgender, 126
Gilligan, C., 156
giving space to feelings, 139
Goldstein, K., 1
Goodman, P., 5, 6, 9, 151, 152, 158
    see also: Friedrich; Posner, L.
Gordon, 25
Gran, S., 25, 161
Greenberg, L. S., 152
group therapy for transgender, 127
guided awareness, 13, 20, 71 see also:
    "experiment"
guided fantasy see also: "experiment"
    betrayal, 39
    to explore relationship, 136–137
guilt and shame, 135

Hahn, T. N., 26, 27
hamster wheel experiment, 32–33
happiness research, 95
Harris, E. S., 154
Healing the Shame that Binds You, 156
Hefferline, R., 5, 6, 9, 151, 152, 158
Helsedirektoratet, 159
here and now, 2, 3, 6, 7, 9, 17 see also:
    "experiment"; I and Thou;
    memories; paradoxical theory
    of change
    being aware of, 20, 72

betrayal, 37–38
bodily sensations, 59
    in therapist, 18–19
    mindfulness and sensing, 46
    relating to each other, 71
    to explore dream image, 47
    to overcome frustration, 142–143
    understanding, 81
    Zeigarnik effect, 8
Hertenstein, M. J., 156
Hjemdal, O. K., 154
Hogg, M. A., 158
holding back, 31, 131, 135, 136, 145–146
holistic awareness, 82–83
Hooks, B., 155
Hopkins, J., 158
Horney, K., 3
Horn, T., 157
Hubble, M. A., 154, 155, 157
humour, 26
Hycner, R., 160

I and Thou, 3, 6, 17, 20 see also:
    here and now
    "awareness", 6
    observe and reflect, 20
    Rubin's vase, 6
I-It, 8, 10, 27 see also: I and Thou
imprisonment purpose not fulfilled,
    74, 79
infidelity, 34, 40
    suspicion after experiencing, 30
inherent factors in person's life, 9
inner dialogue, 7
interaction between language and
    memory, 156
internalised oppression, 10, 63
introjection, 10
I-Thou, 27, 153
    relationships, 8, 10

Jacobs, L., 160
Jacobs, S., 153
Janicki-Deverts, D., 25, 153
Johnson, M., 152, 155
Jørstad, S., 155

Kabat-Zinn, J., 26, 153
Kahn, S. E., 152
Karaniya Metta Sutta, 95
Kardan, O., 153
Keith-Spiege, P., 160
Kellerman, N. P. F., 154
Kellogg, S. H., 152, 159
Kepner, J., 110, 159
Kessler, 25
knowing oneself, 101
knowing other, 18
Koch, C., 155
Kolmannskog, V., 155, 156, 160
Kringlen, E., 156

Lakoff, G., 152, 155
language, role of, 13
Lasch, C., 94, 158
Leibig, A., 151, 161
Levine, P., 159, 161
Levitsky, A., 159
Lewin, K., 8
lifeline approach, 50–55, 56, 65–66
limit of revealing, 82
Lodahl, M. A., 160
Loftus, E. F., 156
love, 149
loving-kindness. *See* metta
Loy, D., 26

Malkin, J., 27
Malt, U., 154
Masson, J., 156
Mathiesen, T., 157
MBCT. *See* mindfulness-based cognitive therapy
MBSR. *See* mindfulness-based stress reduction
meditation, 27 *see also*: metta
memories, 43, 49 *see also*: here and now
   abuse and sexual fantasies, 49–50, 64–65
   adaptation, 45
   communication through reflections, 56
   connection outside of sessions, 59–60, 61
   dissociation, 45, 51, 62–63
   exhale to calm nervous system, 44
   experience of being alone, 44, 61
   exploring dream, 64
   failed therapist, 57
   false memories, 49
   feedback from clients, 66
   feeling the foundation, 43
   flowing together, 58, 61–62
   guiding awareness towards sense, 45
   help from supervisor, 57, 59, 67
   here and now, 47–48, 59
   internalised oppression, 63
   lifeline approach, 50–55, 56, 65–66
   mindfulness and sensing here and now, 46
   opening up to talk, 45
   protest and be respected, 55, 58
   retraumatising, 54
   rituals in therapy, 64
   sexual abuse, 61
   shame, 66
   sharing, 44
   therapy as journey, 63–64
   traumatization, 67
   way to conclude, 46–47
metaphor, 152
   for war, 138
   to understand world, 10
metta, 89–90 *see also*: "experiment"
   for cared one, 140–141
   in self first, 89–90, 91–92, 95
Milde, A. M., 156
Miller, G. E., 25, 153
Miller, S. D., 154, 155, 157
mindfulness, 19, 26–27
   and sensing here and now, 46
mindfulness-based cognitive therapy (MBCT), 26
mindfulness-based stress reduction (MBSR), 26
mind over matter, 70, 80
musts and shoulds, 18

narcissistic culture, 94
nature healing, 27
Neff, K., 159
Neighborhood greenspace and health in large urban center, 153
Nietzsche, 26
Nilsen, J. F., 157
non-judgemental attitude, 26
Norwegian Gestalt Institute, The, 6

observe and reflect, 20
Omland, T., 154
opening up to talk, 45
Øverenget, E., 159

Palmer, J. C., 156
paradoxical theory of change, 8, 74
    see also: gestalt therapy;
    here and now
  accustomed to others, 9
  dialogical relationships, 9
  I-Thou relationship, 8
  response-ability, 9
  therapist as solution, 8
paradox in therapy, 146
patient's state of mind when understood, 132
Pek, J., 159
Perls, F., 6, 9, 14, 41, 64, 18, 150, 151, 152, 156, 158, 159
Perls, L., 5, 150, 151, 161 see also: Posner, L.
  creativity, 5–6
  death, 6
  existential therapy, 5
  moment of fritz' death, 5
  Posner, L. as, 5
person as part of situation, 9
phenomenology, 1
polarity, 11–12
polarization, 87–88
Polster, E., 155
Pope, K. S., 160
Portney, C., 154
Posner, L., 1, 3 see also: Friedrich; Goodman, P.

art and literature, 4
blessing in disguise, 4
family, 4
left South Africa, 4
post-traumatic growth, 150
post-traumatic stress, 40, 121–122
power
  in transgender, 127
  in legs, 150
prayer as medicine, 155
prisoner, 69, 72–73
  adaptation, 73
  aspects in different people, 75
  being aware of here and now, 72
  big boys don't cry, 73, 79, 80
  chair work, 75–77
  feelings surfaced, 73
  guided awareness exercise, 71
  jumping quickly from topic to topic, 69
  mind over matter, 70, 80
  paradoxical theory of change, 74
  polarization, 72, 75
  purpose not fulfilled in imprisonment, 74, 79
  stream of monotonous words, 70–71
  supporting by being quiet, 74
  therapy in semi-open prison, 69
  therapy outcome, 77–78
  wall as contact, 79–80
prison research, 157
production of stress hormones, 25
projected counter-pole, 102
projection, 10, 86–87
protest and be respected, 55, 58
psychological stress and disease, 153
psychology of love, 155
Purser, R., 26
Putnam, F. W., 155
putting words on something wordless, 103–105

reflecting back with client, 19–20
Regjeringen, 160
Reich, W., 3

relational approach, 153
relational meditation, 38
relationship, 10, 18, 25
    building, 82
Resnick, R. W., 156
response-ability, 9
retraumatising, 54
"retroflection", 10–11
rituals in therapy, 64
Roland, E., 157
Roszak, T., 153
Rua, M., 157
Rubin's vase, 2, 6

Salzberg, S., 158
Sandnes, H. E., 157
Sanford, N., 154
sanity, nature of, 153
Satipatthana Sutta, 153
Schei, B., 159
Searles, H. F., 160
secrets and secrecy, 111
self
    and self-image, 93–94
    and shame, 157
    and society, 154
self-esteem and self-compassion, 95–96
self first, 81, 90–91
    "around the world" phenomenon, 94–95
    aware of sensitivity, 88
    being gay, 84
    bullying and homophobia, 93
    chair work, 85–86
    happiness research, 95
    holistic awareness, 82–83
    limit of revealing, 82
    metta, 89–90, 91–92, 95
    narcissistic culture, 94
    outcome, 92
    polarization, 87–88
    projection experiment, 86–87
    relationship building, 82
    self and self-image, 93–94
    self-esteem and self-compassion, 95–96

self-loathing, 84
    whole human beings, 81, 84, 91
selfish, 158
self-loathing, 84
Seligman, M., 158
Selye, H., 25, 153
sex drive in transgender, 120, 124
sexual abuse, 61, 155
shame, 66, 156
sharing, 44
Simkin, J., 151
Skårderud, F., 26, 153
Sloan, R. P., 157
Smith, E. W. L., 151
Smith, P. S., 157
social anxiety in transgender, 115, 116–117, 121
social support, 150
social training for transgender, 123–124
Staemmler, F. M., 155
Stern, D., 155
Stevens, J. O., 152
stress, 17, 20, 25
    relief, 153
stressing less, 19, 23
succeeding at everything, 17
    activities after burnout, 22–23
    burnout, 19, 25
    connecting to breathing, 20
    death perspective on life, 23
    demands exceeding adaptive capacity, 25
    ecopsychology, 27
    existentialism, 25–26
    guided awareness, 20
    humour, 26
    imperfection connecting each other, 22–23
    knowing each other, 18
    meditation, 27
    mindfulness, 19, 26–27
    musts and shoulds, 18
    nature healing, 27
    non-judgemental attitude, 26
    production of stress hormones, 25
    reflecting back with client, 19–20

relations, 25
relationships, 18
stress, 17, 25
stressing less, 19, 23
therapist's impact on client, 24
trust, 21–22
Sue, D. W., 158
Sumerel, M. B., 160
supporting by being quiet, 74
supportive people for transgender, 119, 124

Tabachnik, B. G., 160
Tao, 11
Tedeschi, R. G., 161
therapist
 -client relationship, 3, 10
 as solution, 8
 failed, 57
 impact on client, 24
 love, 138, 145, 146, 147, 148
therapy
 as journey, 63–64
 in prisoner, 77–78
 in self first, 92
 with abused clients, 110
Thoresen, S., 154
Thuen, F., 154
Tomkins, S. S., 156
transformational experiences, 37
transgender, 113, 114, 125
 accepting one another, 123
 becoming rigid, 117
 bravery, 114–115, 117, 122
 changing room, 116
 choice of dress, 120
 denied treatment, 121
 effect of gained attention, 122
 gender identity, 126
 gender-neutral toilets, 116
 gender norms, 127
 gestalt therapy, 126
 group therapy, 127
 liberation, 127
 post-traumatic stress, 121–122
 power, 127
 rage and sorrow, 118
 removed breasts, 116
 sex drive, 120, 124
 situation in Norway, 126
 social anxiety, 115, 116–117, 121
 social training, 123–124
 supportive people, 119, 124
 as unfit parent, 118–119
trauma, 8
 transmission of, 29
traumatization, 67
trust, 21–22
two-chair work, 14

uncertainty and need for control in relationship, 130
understanding the patient, 131
unfaithful, 40
"unfinished business", 8

Valla, B., 157
Van der Ros, J., 159
Vaughan, G. M., 158

Wampold, B. E., 154, 155, 157
Wedge, M., 90
Wheeler, G., 152, 153, 157
whole human beings, 81, 84, 91
wisely selfish, 158

Yalom, I., 155, 160
Yehuda, R., 154
yin and yang, 11
Yontef, G., 156, 157, 158
Yu, Y., 161

Zeigarnik, B., 8, 152
Zeigarnik effect, 8
Zen, 3–4, 70
Zinker, J., 12, 94, 149, 152, 158, 160

Milton Keynes UK
Ingram Content Group UK Ltd.
UKHW021913310823
427868UK00011B/108